Th

The Poet and the Landscape

THE POET AND THE LANDSCAPE

Andrew Young

RUPERT HART-DAVIS
Soho Square London
1962

PRINTED IN GREAT BRITAIN BY
WESTERN PRINTING SERVICES LIMITED, BRISTOL

DEDICATED

by kind permission

TO

HER ROYAL HIGHNESS

Princess Alexandra of Kent

Contents

8   *Contents*

Two of these pieces, "Haworth" and "The Tweed," appeared some time ago in a book of mine called *A Prospect of Britain*, which is now out of print. All the others appear here for the first time.

A.Y.

Windsor

THE CASTLE

IF we follow the servants who carried Falstaff in a buck-basket to Datchet Mead, we shall have our best view of Windsor Castle. We shall see it better for not seeing it well, distance hiding much that is prosaic, nineteenth-century masonry and false Gothic. It is stretched out its full eventful length, high on a chalk hill, so high that the foliage of trees lies in great wreaths about its base. The outline is majestic as though cut to a pattern on the sky; royal as a postage stamp, it inspires a belief in the divine right of kings.

> A nobler weight no mountain bears,
> But Atlas only, which supports the spheres.[1]

Cupid and the Muses could not have conspired to find a fitter scene for a king's love-poem. The king was James I of Scotland, who as a boy,

> Not far passit the state of innocence,

was taken from a ship on his way to France, and spent part of a long captivity in a tower of Windsor Castle.

> Now was there maid fast by the Touris wall
> A garden faire, and in the corneris set
> Ane herbere greene.

On this he could look down, and there for the first time

---

[1] Denham, *Cooper's Hill.*

no doubt he heard the nightingale. Scottish poets have strange notions of this English bird; Dunbar says its feathers "as the pacock shone," and Sir David Lindsay that its voice "redoundid through the mountains." It must have been a matter of curious interest to the young prince to see and hear for himself "the lytil suete nyghtingale." The bird's song was the prelude to summer:

> "Worschippe, ye that loveris bene, this May,
>   For of your bliss the kalendis are begonne,
> And sing with us, away, winter, away,
>   Come somer, come, the suete seson and sonne."

But the song was the prelude to another "bliss" and "suete seson," for the prince was to fall in love with the lady walking in the garden,

> the freschest younge floure
> That ever I sawe, methought, before that houre;
> For which sodayne abate, anon astert
> The blude of all my body to my hert.

The lady was Jane Beaufort, young daughter of the Earl of Somerset. Scotland had to pay 60,000 marks for her young king's release, or, as the English government preferred to put it, for his nurture and education during eighteen years. The sum was enormous, but he took back to Scotland a wife, and with her a poem or, as he calls it, a book, *The Kingis Quhair.*

THE RIVER

So noble is the view of the royal castle, roof and turret and tower, that it seems almost disrespectful to speak of the view from it. It is not as impressive as the famous view from Richmond Hill, which Thomson hails: "O Vale of Bliss! — O softly spreading Hills! — Heavens! — Happy

BRITANNIA!"; but it ranges far and wide, extensive
as a view from an aeroplane. We look down on Windsor,
but not in the sense Swift did, when he wrote to Stella,
"the town is scoundrel"; it is a town of some distinction.
And, of course, there is the river. The Thames is not a
great river as rivers go; but we may feel it is, for, as
Lucretius said, thinking no doubt of the smaller Tiber,
"Any river is huge to him who has seen no greater." Yet
at Windsor it has no spectacular bank as at Cliveden Reach
higher up, where dark unchanging yews mock its incessant
flow; nor has it even the sweep with which lower down it
approaches Richmond Hill. It leaves the Castle to dominate
the scene, content to fling a paternal arm round Eton
College. Perhaps it is overawed by the Castle, for out of its
sight it plucks up spirit, so that Old Windsor, which you
expect to be a decayed place, has a surprisingly gay
appearance.

From Windsor Castle Charles II issued to fish near
Datchet; he came home laden with gudgeon, but failed to
learn from them the lesson that he might be a fish himself
to his flattering courtiers. So at least an unknown poet
suggests:

> Nor is he warned by their unhappy fate;
> But greedily he swallows every bait,
> A prey to every king-fisher of state.

And from Eton College Sir Henry Wotton came across the
meadow to fish. Provost of Eton, he was a man of great
learning; Cowley says he knew so many languages that

> He had (you'd swear)
> Not only *Liv'd*, but *been Born* every where,

and had mastered every subject,

And when he sawe that he through all had past
He *dy'd*, lest he should *Idle* grow at last.

The art of angling was not an exception. But he may not
have been as successful as his friend Isaak Walton, who
says, "There is in the *Thames* about *Windsor*, a little trout
called a Samlet, or Skegger Trout; in which place I have
caught twenty or forty at a standing." He could say of
Walton,

> There stood my friend, with patient skill
> Attending of his trembling quill,

but his own eyes seem to have wandered from his trembling
quill. At least so one imagines from *On a Bank as I Sat
Fishing*:

> JOAN takes the neat-rubb'd pail, and now
> She trips to milk the sand-red Cow;
> Where, for some sturdy foot-ball swain,
> She strokes a syllabub or twain.

THE FOREST

One thing we miss from the Castle view is Windsor
Forest. When the Earl of Surrey looked out from his "so
cruell prison," he saw in sad memory

> Where we did chace the fearfull hart a force.

The hart, not the fox; he hoped no one would think him
so light

> Nor of so chorlish kind
> That I would leave the hind
> To hunt the gander's fo.

But if forest means wild open country, it can hardly be
applied to the Great Park, still less to the Little, now

called the Home. No one sees in these pleasances what
Surrey saw with the coming of summer,

> The hart hath hong his olde hed on the pale;
> The buck in brake his winter cote he flings.

One might say that Pope's poem is the only *Windsor Forest*.
Pope had not reached the satirical stage when he could
say,

> Woods are—not to be too prolix—
> Collective bodies of straight sticks.

He writes of them with charm:

> Here waving boughs a chequered scene display,
> And part admit, and part exclude the day;
> As some coy nymph her lover's warm address
> Nor quite indulges, nor can quite repress.

Perhaps the comparison is less suggestive of woodland
solitude than of "the dear, damn'd, distracting town"; but
young Pope had a true eye for country sights.

> See! from the brake the whirring pheasant springs;

the exclamatory "See!" is hardly needed; the pheasant's
flight is clear enough. We notice, too,

> His purple crest, and scarlet-circled eyes.

Pope's ear is even truer; it might have been of his verse he
was thinking when he said,

> Nor rivers winding through the vales below,
> So sweetly warble, or so smoothly flow.

Handel set to music the lines beginning, "Where'er you
walk." The idea! The "little nightingale" had his own
music.

Cleveland Moors

PERHAPS no part of England has preserved so well its prehistoric appearance as the Cleveland moors. That is best appreciated when the dales are out of sight, for they have changed. Once thickly wooded, mostly with pine and oak, they must have looked from the moors like underground forests; it was said that a squirrel could travel from Commondale to Glaisdale, a distance of eight miles, without touching the ground. Now they are mostly under cultivation with alders and willows growing meditatively by the becks. But the moors appear to have remained untouched except for the few inevitable roads. That they have been unploughed has saved their antiquities, and these in particular give them their unusual prehistoric appearance. Round barrows, called by the local Norse name "howes," mainly of the Mid-Bronze Age, everywhere catch the eye. And what else is there to catch the eye on these empty moors? Camden could still say, "Among the Mountains of Blackamore there is nothing remarkable." There is only a wide waste of heather, for whose dull brown monotony the plant will blush in August. All is so primeval, you become more than a prehistorian, prehistoric yourself. But now a great change is taking place; over the moors are marching those armies that do not march, conifer plantations. Cleveland will look as though it had been turned upside down, the dales clear of trees and the forests on the moors.

The red grouse, being our only endemic species of bird, has a peculiar right to the moors, if only the sad right to be shot down on them; the dingy grey sheep, whose hoofs and droppings have made their grassy paths, have also a claim, and are so much a part of the landscape that they look like moving rocks; for the sake of these, no doubt, a substantial amount of the moors will be preserved. But much will be lost, much more than their antiquities. We shall lose the sense of vast space which gives them, barren and featureless as they are, a touch of the sublime. The hills, many of which have "Moor" as part of their name, can so little interrupt the view that the effect is of an enormous tableland. Of course the flatness is deceptive, for there are long intervening dales, over which the eye takes a blind leap. The sense of space is helped by a remarkable lack of incident, such as house or tree. On a hazy day particularly the moors stretch to infinitude. Some Pennine moors look as if they filled half of England, but these moors exhaust heaven itself, which bends down to bring them to an end. The loneliness of it all creates distance of another kind, a remoteness from the world's affairs. "Live as on a mountain," says Marcus Aurelius; you could not live better on a mountain than on these flat moors.

Yet it is not of an empty space you may be aware; the wild sombre character of the moors and their antiquities, these in combination, charge it with a weird, even heathenish atmosphere. Nothing haunts barrows on the placid chalk hills of the South, but many of these howes have a name, such as Elf, Hob and Old Wife. Old Wife may have been Bel, Wade's wife. That giant made the road across the moors, Wade's Causey, in order that dryshod she might drive her cows. Certainly he had no need for a road himself, for as Chaucer's Ianuarie knew, he had a magic

B

boat in which he could fly. "Concerning Wade and his
bote, as also his straunge exploits in the same, because the
matter is long and fabulous, I pass it over." But travellers,
knowing the matter, could not lightly pass it over; before
venturing on the moors they would open the door of
Pickering Church and take a look at another giant, St
Christopher, the protector against sudden death, painted
on the wall. A more sinister figure than Bel was Bride,
after whom the uncanny stones on Pickering Moor are
named. She was the Celtic goddess of fertility, but a bridal
couple, who went out to the stones to spend their first
night together, were never again seen. Though serving
another purpose, as to show a road or boundary, the many
stone crosses on the moors must have been a comfort to
pilgrims on their way to Whitby or some other shrine. Yet
even stone crosses, standing in lonely places and seen in a
strange light, can look peculiar, and having names like the
two on Rosedale Head might become animate; "when
Ralph Cross and Fat Betty meet, there will be a wedding."
What with one thing and another the moors have an atmosphere that makes it easy to believe that Ritson was right
in associating with Cleveland the *Lyke-Wake Dirge*,

> This ae nighte, this ae nighte,
> Every nighte and alle;
> Fire and fleet and candle-lighte,
> And Christe receive thye saule.

Lustingham Church, just off the moors, has a remarkable
crypt; its Norman pillars with ram's-horn capitals, ancient
stones and layout as of an underground church, make it
one of the most singular buildings in England; the steps
leading down to it take you deep into the past, where you
breathe an atmosphere that goes slightly to the head. The

Lyke-Wake Dirge produces something of that effect. It was
sung at funerals: "when any dieth, certaine women sing a
song to the dead bodie, recyting the jorney that the partye
deceased must goe."

> When thou from hence away art past,
>   Every nighte and alle;
> To Whinny-muir thou com'st at laste;
>   And Christe receive thye saule.

Alms the deceased had given will benefit him here, "for as
much, as after this life, he has to pass barefoote through a
great launde, full of thornes and furzen, except by the
meryte of the almes aforesaid they have redemed the
forfeyte."

> If ever thou gavest hosen and shoon,
>   Every nighte and alle;
> Sit thee down and put them on;
>   And Christe receive thye saule.

After Whinny-muir the soul comes to the Brig o' Dread.
It is not as hopeless as that bridge in *Death's Jest-Book*—

> We walk on ice
> Over the mouth of Hell—

for what it leads to is Purgatory fire. Here again alms-
giving will profit the soul:

> If ever thou gavest meate or drinke,
>   Every nighte and alle;
> The fire sall never make thee shrink;
>   And Christe receive thy saule.

> If meate or drink thou ne'er gav'st nane,
>   Every nighte and alle;
> The fire will burn thee to the bare bane;
>   And Christe receive thy saule.

Whether Ritson was right or not, this ancient poem with its stark statement and habit of repetition has a correspondence with these bare monotonous moors. But it will not last long; the conifers are taking possession of the land. When their funeral processions set out, the dead trunks lying stiff and straight, no one will sing a *Lyke-Wake Dirge*. And there will be no compensation for the loss of the wild scene, as there is in North Cleveland, now an industrial district with a ruined landscape. There the compensation may seem greater than the loss. Nowhere in England, perhaps in the world, is there a grander sight than Middlesbrough's blast furnaces by night, a lurid glow in the darkness with now and then a tall shooting flame that lightens and alarms the clouds. It is the best English translation of Dante's *Inferno*.

The Medway Valley

FULLER in his *Worthies of England* makes the pleasant
remark about Kent, "it differeth not more from other
shires than from itself, such the variety thereof." To this
variety the Medway Valley makes a rich contribution, for
not only does it differ from the rest of Kent, it differs from
itself, Ashdown Forest at one end being unlike the
Hundred of Hoo at the other, and both unlike the gap
through the chalk Downs. Yet it is a kind of country by
itself, unless there are two countries, divided by the river,
the Kentish Men to the west, the Men of Kent to the east.
And it has everything a civilised country should have, such
as megaliths on an impressive scale, as at Coldrum and
Kit's Coty, and Roman remains. At Offam is the only
quintain in England, usually mistaken for a signpost. With
a waterway running far inland it could not fail to have its
own old history; that, indeed, is suggested by the Kentish
Men claiming to be descended from the Saxons and the
Men of Kent from their enemies, the Jutes. And of course
it has given birth to famous men, one in particular, Sir
Philip Sidney. Fulke Greville was speaking not only for
England but for most of Europe when he described him as
"the wonder of our age" and "the world's delight." For
young Shakespeare, who was born the year Philip entered
Shrewsbury School, he must have been an object of hero-
worship; and afterwards it is not unlikely that he copied
him in his picture of Hamlet:

The courtier's, soldier's, scholar's, eye, tongue, sword;
The expectancy and rose of the fair state,
The glass of fashion and the mould of form,
The observed of all observers.

The Medway Valley is not a small country; bounded by low hills, it has the appearance of a wide plain. If the river lies in a narrow bed, it occupies a large bedroom. Not till it reaches Nettlestead with its old barn and fifteenth-century church glass do you have the feeling of a valley. So it is from there you can most pleasantly follow the river—it will not keep up with you!—to the neighbourhood of Maidstone, pausing perhaps on the medieval bridges at Teston and East Farleigh. Yet it is not in itself an attractive river.

The liquid serpent draws its silver train,

says Sir Richard Blackmore; but it is not silver, but brown, the water so muddy that to compare it with beer would be an insult to the hop-gardens. Also it is slow and dumb. Yet why should it not delay in so sweet a country? In apple-blossom time, when every tree is its own blush, one wonders at the modesty of the title, Garden of England; why not, when one is thinking of apples anyhow, Garden of Eden?

Hops, however, are not so suggestive of the Garden of Eden as apples, and they are more characteristic of the Medway Valley. Oast-houses with their steep conical roofs and white ventilating caps make Kent more readily recognisable than any other part of England. That is fortunate, for few functional buildings have such charm; they startle the eye by their odd shape and yet fit admirably into the landscape. They have a somewhat weird look on dark autumn nights, when lights glitter through chinks as from an infernal fire. The experienced hop-drier is at work,

stirring the sulphurous furnace. If Bacchus is the god of
hops, as Christopher Smart says,[1] Courthope describes the
burnt-offering:

> From the moist flowers the drowsy fumes ascend,
> Rush through the cowl to mingle with the day,
> And in blue vapour breathe their weight away.[2]

The Medway Valley has provided poets with scenes,
notably Tennyson, who stayed with his married sister
Cecilia at Park House near Maidstone, and Spenser, who
for a time was secretary to the Bishop of Rochester. At
Park House Tennyson wrote *The Princess*, laying the scene
of the opening fête in its grounds. Though the main action
takes place in an imaginary country, it may owe something
to the wooded park; there is nothing imaginary in the
image,

> the golden autumn woodland reels
> Athwart the smoke of burning weeds.

Tennyson saw it with a clear eye, unaffected by the smoke.
The Downs above the Medway are the scene of Spenser's
Shepheardes Calender; but he makes little of them; his
characters, who speak with a northern accent, might almost
as well be in their own country. Yet he realised the importance of the Medway, pausing in *The Faerie Queene* to give
a long account of its marriage with the Thames:

> Then came the Bride, the lovely *Medua* came.

The dull river's loveliness must have been due to the dress,

> That seem'd like silver, sprinckled here and theare
> With glittering spangs, that did like starres appeare.

Perhaps Spenser had seen a low sun striking sparks from

---

[1] *The Hop-Garden.*   [2] *Hop-Picking.*

the muddy estuary. Among the wedding guests were the Nile, Euphrates, Ganges and even the Amazon. The Medway is a more important river than most people imagine.

At Penshurst Place on the Upper Medway young Philip Sidney entertained his literary friends, in particular the two poets of whom he says,

> My two and I be met,
> A happy blessed trinitie.

One was Sir Edward Dyer, whose fame depends mainly on the line,

> My mind to me a kingdom is,

the first line of a poem to which the rest does not live up, though he may have lived up to it himself. The other was Fulke Greville, afterwards Lord Brooke, whose name is better known, at least to Londoners, for he left it to the street in which he was murdered, Brook Street. They were patriotic in an unusual way, inspired by the ambition that English poetry should equal, if not surpass, the poetry of "that sweet enemy, France." It was their kind of talk that Richard Crashaw asked of his mistress, "that not impossible she":

> *Sydnaean* showers
> Of sweet discourse, whose powers
> Can crown old Winter's head with flowers.

The request itself was not impossible, for it appears that Mary, Philip's sister—was she the first English woman writer?—took a full share in the conversation. Certainly she was an accomplished lady according to William Browne's famous *Epitaph*:

Underneath this sable Herse
Lyes the subject of all verse:
Sydney's Sister, Pembroke's Mother:
Death, ere thou hast slaine another,
Faire, and Learn'd, and good as she,
Time shall throw a dart at thee.

Even after Philip's death, his brother reigning there, Penshurst Place was a resort of poets. That Ben Jonson enjoyed its hospitality we have his word:

Here no man tells my cups; nor, standing by,
A waiter, doth my gluttony envy.

And Ben was a stout trencherman if his mistress, as he says,

Read so much waist, as she cannot imbrace
My mountaine belly.

But Sir Robert could afford to be hospitable, for as Ben pointed out to him in his poem *To Penshurst,*

The painted partrich lyes in every field,
And, for thy messe, is willing to be kill'd;
And if the high swolne *Medway* faile thy dish
Thou hast thy ponds, that pay thee tribute fish,
Fat, aged carps, that runne into thy net,
And pikes, now weary their owne kinde to eat,
Bright eeles, that emulate them, and leape on land,
Before the fisher, or into his hand.

At a later time Edmund Waller was a guest, for at Penshurst Place he wooed young Lady Dorothea Sidney, to whom he gave the sugary name Sacharissa. Though the Medway was grieved she refused him—

The crystal waters weep away,
And bear the tidings to the sea[1]—

[1] Christopher Smart, *Ode on Saint Cecilia's Day.*

perhaps she was wise. When later in life she asked, "When will you write such verses on me again?" he gave the ungracious reply, "When you are as young, madam, and as handsome as you were then."

But the Medway Valley has had its own poets, among them Christopher Smart. Born prematurely, writing poems at the age of four, eloping at the age of thirteen with a girl younger than himself, he appears to have been somewhat precocious. So it is not surprising that before leaving the Medway Valley at the age of eleven, he had already developed the love for it that lasted through his life. At Shipbourne, too, his heart may have begun to warm to the small creatures of which he had afterwards so much to say, the birds:

> Blessed be the name of the Lord Jesus against the destruction of Small Birds;

and the fish,

> Which nature frames of light escape,
> Devouring man to shun;

and even the glow-worm, "who is a living mineral." But his chief affection was for flowers,

> For Flowers are peculiarly the poetry of Christ;

the Lily still smiles to think it was mentioned in the Sermon on the Mount. Flowers are as good as animals,

> For Flowers can see, and Pope's Carnations knew him.

Of course no flower could be as good as his cat Jeoffry,

> For he purrs in thankfulness, when God tells him he's a good cat.

All these creatures,

> And apples of ten thousand tribes,
> And quick peculiar quince,

were created for one purpose, ADORATION. So, too, was the little bibulous man, Kit Smart. "My poor friend Smart showed the disturbance of his mind," said Dr Johnson, "by falling on his knees, and saying his prayers in the street, or in any other unusual place." But he was only following the apostolic injunction, "Pray without ceasing." And he was right to insist his friends should join him in his prayers, dragging them out of their beds or breaking up convivial parties. That he was put in a madhouse was to Kit religious persecution. But perhaps it was also providential; without the seven temperate years in confinement he might not have written *A Song to David*.

Where Sir Charles Sedley was born is uncertain, but part of his youth was spent at the Friary, just below Aylesford Bridge. The conventual air of the place hardly suggests the home of a notorious rake. His spontaneous poems express his light character:

> Phillis is my only Joy,
> Faithless as the Winds or Seas;

but we get to know him also in his friend Etherege's comedy, *The Man of Mode, or, Sir Fopling Flutter*, where Medley is no doubt Sedley. Emilia says of him, "Y'are a living Libel, a breathing Lampoon," and Dorimant refers to his habit of getting "rhetorically drunk." Perhaps he gave the chief display of his rhetoric when, standing naked on the balcony of the Cock Tavern in London, he preached a mock sermon in the Puritan style to about a thousand people. Milton may not have slept through that sermon, for it caused a considerable outcry, stones thrown from the road and bottles from the balcony. What is not unlikely at

least is that he refers to Sedley and his associates in
Paradise Lost, which he was writing about that time:

> when night
> Darkens the streets, then wander forth the sons
> Of Belial flown with insolence and wine.

Harriet in *The Man of Mode* loved London to such a degree
that, as she said, "I can scarce indure the Country in
Landscapes and in Hangings." Probably Sedley's feeling
for town and country was not much different. When he had
occasion to refer to the Medway Valley, it was to Rochester
he referred; there, wakened too early by a crowing cock,
he expressed the unkindly wish,

> May rivals tread thy Hens before thy Face.

Sir Thomas Wyatt, born at Allington Castle near Maidstone, a castle wonderfully restored from being a ruin,
shows at least some feeling for country life. Much of his
time was spent at Henry VIII's court, and when that
monarch was troubled about getting the Pope's consent to
his divorce from Catharine, he must have been pleased
with the witty remark, "Lord! that a man cannot repent
of his sin without the Pope's leave." Also, a good scholar
and linguist—he went to Cambridge at the age of twelve—
Wyatt was often abroad on diplomatic missions. Yet there
were times when he was happy to say,

> But here am I in Kent and Christendome
> Emong the muses where I rede and ryme.

The popular phrase, "Kent and Christendom," is odd
coming from a Kentish man, for according to a note to the
Shepheardes Calender it implies that Kent is outside the
Christian pale. One wonders what the Bishop of Rochester
thought of the note. While Wyatt's only apparent interest

in the Medway Valley was in hunting, sometimes with
bow and arrow, his reading and rhyming had a far-reaching
result; he imported the sonnet from the Continent. Though
he stutters in his own sonnets, being more fluent in other
forms of verse, Allington Castle is the source of all the
great English sonnet-sequences, from Sidney's *Astrophel
and Stella* to Meredith's *Modern Love*.

That is the Medway Valley's only claim on the sonnet-
sequence first to be written, if not first to be published; we
have no reason to suppose it was written at Penshurst
Place. There Sidney could have heard the nightingale "a
thorne her song-booke making," but he might have heard
it in London; nightingales sing in Shirley's *Hyde Park*.
And the Medway Valley has no claim to be the scene of his
meetings with Stella; London is a likelier place. In any case
we do not know that the incidents recorded are autobiographical. Fulke Greville says the poems "were scrib-
bled rather as pamphlets, for the entertainment of time, and
friends, than any account of himself to the world." Nashe
in a preface described it as "a tragicomedy of love as
played out by starlight." Even the title, *Astrophel and
Stella*, *Star-lover and Star*, might suggest that all his love
amounted to was

> The desire of the moth for the star.

One might hope it did not amount to much more, for Stella
in her later years was a fallen star. Perhaps she had already
begun to fall when he wrote in the final sonnet,

> Leave me, O Love, which reachest but to dust.

Shakespeare's Flowers

THE Fairy in *A Midsummer Night's Dream*, speaking of cowslips, says to Puck,

> In their gold coats spots you see.

Insects see these spots, for they are honey-guides, aids to identifying a flower with nectar; Ariel, too, sees them, for he says,

> In the cowslip's bell I lie;

but Puck may not have seen them, for they are not readily noticed unless the flower is picked and held in the hand. No doubt Shakespeare picked cowslips as a child. He would also pick primroses; they were much admired; in Thenot's fable a conceited rose-tree claims to be the primrose of the land.[1] Sometimes they cross with cowslips to produce hybrids, "tall oxlips"; these he would pick, and "azured harebells," which were probably bluebells. Perhaps he stuck flowers in his cap like the soldiers in *Macbeth*.

As a boy he may have gathered burs, the sticky purple flower-heads of burdocks; they were so plentiful that Celia says, "if we walk not in the trodden paths, our very petticoats will catch them." But they may have caught them in the Stratford-on-Avon streets, boys throwing burs at girls, for this, we also gather from Celia, was "a holiday foolery." Perhaps he went into the woods for pignuts, so named because pigs root them up and they have a nutty

[1] Spenser, *The Shepheardes Calender.*

flavour. He could have eaten them raw or taken them home
for his mother to toast. The plant's white flower would
show where they were, well beneath the soil's surface, as
he remembered when he made Caliban say, "I with my
long nails will dig thee pignuts." With the tuberous roots
of another plant he was acquainted, at least by hearsay, the
early purple orchid's; Hamlet's mother, confusing flowers
with roots, calls them

> long purples,
> That liberal shepherds give a grosser name,
> But our cold maids do dead men's fingers call them.

That Shakespeare makes her refer to the grosser name,
unnecessary and unbecoming in a queen, suggests he was
recalling how to his adolescent companions, if not to
himself, it was the subject of a vulgar joke.

But he must have grown up to take a practical interest
in plants; he would see them in his father's house,

> for every man
> Was his own patient and physician.[1]

They were cut and dried, as we say of plans, if no longer of
plants, or transmuted into tinctures, juleps, boluses, electu-
aries or what not. They were mostly simples, as contrasted
with compounds which, like the melancholy of Jaques,
were compounded of many simples, extracted from many
objects. Friar Laurence in *Romeo and Juliet* held that all
plants could serve as simples,

> Many for many virtues excellent,
> None but for some, and yet all different;

and, sure enough, in the Apothecary's shop Romeo saw
even "old cakes of roses."

[1] William Browne, *Britannia's Pastorals.*

A rose, besides his beauty, is a cure.[1]

The most unlikely plants were medicinal for, as Northumberland points out, "in poison there is physic." People had great faith in herbs; had they not the word of Scripture, "the Lord created medicines out of the earth"? But there was also scepticism; when physicians

> Seek out for plants with signatures,
> To quack of universal cures,

they are as likely to kill as to cure according to Butler's *Hudibras*. Shakespeare had no doubt read in the famous *Essays* Montaigne's answer to those who urged him to take physic, "at least let them tarry till such time as I have recovered my health and strength." He may no more have shared Friar Laurence's faith in herbs than Marston shared Dulcimel's belief, "in China, when women are past child-bearing, they are all burnt to make gun-powder."

Plants had an index to the ailments they cured;

> by some Signature
> Nature herself doth point us out a cure.[2]

Julius Caesar might have saved himself from swooning in the market-place, as Casca describes, if he had known that mistletoe, by hanging down from a bough, showed it was a cure for the falling sickness. To us some signatures may not appear very legible, that a plantain has prostrate leaves and its name is derived from the Latin *planta*, sole of the foot, seems hardly a sufficient reason for Costard and Romeo taking it to be the cure for a broken shin. But a signature might be the index to something quite different from a cure; knotgrass by its habit of stifling other plants

[1] George Herbert.
[2] William Browne, *Britannia's Pastorals*.

indicated that it hindered growth. This made it useful for thieves who needed a small accomplice to break into a house; so Dorothy says to Tinker in *The Coxcomb*,

> We want a boy extremely for this function,
> Kept under for a year with milk and knotgrass.[1]

Naturally Hermia's parents fed her with milk, but the faithless Lysander suggests they gave her something else:

> Get you gone, you dwarf,
> You minimus, of hindering knotgrass made.

Certainly she was short, for Helena can say to her,

> My legs are longer though, to run away.

Indeed, this Doctrine of Signatures, as it was called, was not an unmixed blessing; providence also seemed to favour thieves in the case of fern-seed. Ferns have no seeds, but they produce spores, which develop into tiny grass-like plants and these in turn, being hermaphrodites, create ferns; as someone has said, ferns have no parents, only grandparents. But these powdery spores were thought to be seeds, and as they were too small to be separately visible, they had the magic power of Gyges' ring or Perseus' cap. To Gadshill it made highway robbery so safe that he could say, "We steal as in a castle, cock-sure; we have the receipt of fern-seed." Even Falstaff, his accomplice, fat as he was, would be invisible.

There were other plants with dramatic possibilities, such as moonwort, which was also a providential gift to thieves;

> Trust not a woman, they have found the herb
> To open locks.[2]

[1] Beaumont and Fletcher.
[2] Shirley, *The Constant Maid.*

Shakespeare makes little use of them, even of the famous mandrake, though the fact that its name begins with "man" suggested great possibilities. Perhaps its longer name, mandragora, had a lulling sound for him, for he associates the plant with sleep: "not poppy or mandragora." Cleopatra must have regarded it as a wonderful soporific:

> Give me to drink mandragora,
> That I might sleep out this great gap of time
> My Antony is away.

She would drink it as a wine called morion. But it was not to produce sleep that Rachel said to Leah, "Give me, I pray thee, of thy son's mandrakes"; on the contrary, it was to produce children. But the mandrakes sold in London for that purpose were only the large roots of bryony carved to look like little men. It was these Falstaff had in mind when he said to his Page, "Thou whoreson mandrake, thou art fitter to be worn in my cap than to wait at my heels." Very different was the true mandrake if, as Cowley says,

> This Monster struck Bellona's self with awe,
> When first the Man-resembling plant she saw.

Shakespeare knows, of course, that the mandrake offers a vocal protest against being pulled out of the ground, but seems doubtful as to the sound's nature; Juliet speaks of it as a shriek, Suffolk as a groan. Perhaps it could be either, for Donne appeals to Love,

> Make me a mandrake, so I may groane here,

while Vittoria Corombona says,

> Millions are now in graves, which at last day
> Like mandrakes shall rise shrieking.[1]

[1] Webster, *The White Devil.*

No poet of the time could have failed to take an interest in emblematic plants.

> The marigold that goes to bed with the sun,
> And with him rises weeping,

was popular with poets; its habit of turning, even of bending to the sun, due to the stem's shaded side growing faster than the other, made it an emblem of devoted love. As it has now been replaced in gardens by the chrysanthemum, so camomile has been driven out of lawns by grass and the introduction of the lawn-mower. "Camomile the more it is trodden on the faster it grows." That made it the emblem of patient love:

> For ne'er was simple camomile so trod on,
> Yet still I grow in love.[1]

But perhaps Falstaff was wrong about it growing faster; he may have been misled by the stronger scent released by the treading. This scent is due to a volatile oil, helpful to the plant, as it mitigates the sun's rays and serves to keep it fresh. Several plants, native to the hot dry Mediterranean coast, having such an oil, were grown in English gardens for their freshness and scent. Rosemary is so much a plant of the coast that its name means Dew of the Sea. Almost an everlasting, keeping

> Seeming and savour all the winter long,

it was an emblem of undying love. As such it was suitable for a wedding or a funeral. Herrick addresses *The Rosemarie Branch* in his garden,

> Grow for two ends, it matters not at all,
> Be't for my *Bridall*, or my *Buriall*.

[1] Shirley, *Hyde Park*.

These uses are in strange contrast: Venturewell wants for his daughter's wedding "a good piece of beef stuck with rosemary";[1] to Juliet's sorrowing parents and friends the Friar says

> Dry up your tears, and stick your rosemary
> On this fair corse.

Rue had too bitter a scent to be associated with weddings; the Gardener in *King Richard II* plants it

> In the remembrance of a weeping queen.

With it was associated wormwood, but less bitter than rue it could serve a practical purpose. The Nurse put it on her dug to wean Juliet. It is surprising she needed it, for according to the Nurse's calculation she was in her fourth year. She might have fulfilled the prophet's saying, "The sucking child shall play on the hole of the asp."

Apart from emblematic plants Shakespeare's references to garden flowers, though frequent, are apt to be casual;

> lilies of all kinds,
> The flower-de-luce being one,

Perdita says briefly, while over the wild flowers she lingers.

> Violets dim,
> But sweeter than the lids of Juno's eyes
> Or Cytherea's breath;

it is unlikely violets were grown in gardens, where exotic plants were much affected; in the frontispiece of his *Herbal* Gerald is shown holding in his hand the potato.

> Daffodils,
> That come before the swallow dares, and take
> The winds of March with beauty,

[1] Beaumont and Fletcher, *The Knight of the Burning Pestle.*

these are surely the small fluttering daffodils of the open champaign, commoner in his time, not the "brass bands" of sheltered gardens. That he shared Perdita's feeling for the wild flowers is suggested by the curious case of love-in-idleness, commonly called heart's-ease. Poets usually write best about flowers when they refer to them in a general way:

> All the flowers of the spring
> Meet to perfume our burying;[1]

in Shakespeare there is often value in a particular reference.

I know a bank where the wild thyme blows;

though all the flowers called love-in-idleness are purple with love's wound, Oberon marks the one "where the bolt of Cupid fell." But what is curious is that while he sees it in a wood near Athens, he speaks of it as "a little western flower." Clearly it is Shakespeare who speaks; his mind may be in that far eastern wood, but his heart for the moment is back in a Warwickshire lane.

[1] Webster, *The Devil's Law-Case.*

"*Poly-Olbion*"

Poly-Olbion is little less, though a great deal more, than a gazetteer of Britain. Wales for its size occupies a large place in the poem, while Scotland is nowhere. Certainly Drayton would not have agreed with Dr Johnson: "Wales is so little different from England, that it offers nothing to the speculation of the traveller." There were the mountains, of which he was a great admirer, perhaps the first English poet to admire them at all;

The Mountaine is the King!

That was true of Snowdon, which in the map he must have used, Saxton's, is four miles high! And for him the Welsh were the true Britons; not only that,

the Britan is so naturallie infus'd
With true Poetick rage,

his small country deserved generous treatment from a poet. Probably Drayton would not have agreed with another opinion of Dr Johnson: "Seeing Scotland, Madam, is only seeing a worse England." He intended to continue the poem,

Till through the sleepy Maine to *Thuly* I have gone,
And seen the frozen Iles;

by the sleepy Main he means the stormy Pentland Firth and by the frozen Iles the Shetlands which, favoured by the Atlantic drift, have about the same winter temperature as

London. Why he failed to finish the work we do not know; some people may think a poem of about 15,000 lengthy lines is long enough.

Poly-Olbion is less than a gazetteer for being a poem. That it is in verse does not matter greatly, as for long stretches the verse falls little short of prose. But naturally the treatment of its subject is less systematic than a gazetteer's. Yet it may be suitable for England, for the land itself is unsystematic. No other country in Europe shows as great a geologic variety in as small a compass. Scenic changes can be sudden and surprising; the spectator may be unable to choose between two charming views as Ovid between his two mistresses: "the one is fairer than the other—and the other is also fairer than she; one pleases me more—and so does the other, too!" And while a gazetteer usually keeps to main roads, *Poly-Olbion* follows winding rivers and even streams. It is both "Geographicall and Hydrographicall." That again may suit a country which excels in the number of its rivers and streams. And it gives us a sight of what motorists miss: "delicate embroidered Meadowes, often veined with gentle gliding Brookes; in which thou maist fully view the dainty Nymphes in their simple naked bewties, bathing in the Crystalline streames." And there is not a gazetteer's emphasis on big towns. If admiration for these has to be shown, it is left to a passing river to show it; at Gloucester the Severn divides itself to get a completer view of the city, and at Shrewsbury it winds about as unwilling to leave the town. The river, of course, is simple-minded;

A Citie's but a sinke, gay houses gawdy graves.

Poly-Olbion is more than a gazetteer by including with other things natural history. Drayton gives a list of birds

in his native Warwickshire, adding a note, "Of all Birds
only the *Blackbird* whistleth." The others are vocal enough;

> even the ecchoing Ayre
> Seemes all compos'd of sounds.

His interest extends to fishes, even to the one-eyed fish
that swims in the Snowdon tarns. He describes how a
leaping salmon

> His taile takes in his teeth; and bending like a bow,
>   That's to a compasse drawn, aloft himself doth throwe;

Giraldus Cambrensis gives the same account in his *Itinerary
of Wales*. To his list of wild plants he adds garden flowers.
Though the most mythological of poets, he does not
mention Flora; she had become the goddess of artificial
flowers. He speaks of the medicinal uses of herbs; perhaps
he learned them from John Hall, Shakespeare's son-in-law,
a doctor who cured him of a tertian fever with a syrup of
violets. His most remarkable tree is what Gerald calls
"Goosetree, Barnacle tree, or tree bearing Geece."
Drayton describes how the fruits ripen

> untill you well may see
> Them turn'd to perfect Fowles, when dropping from the tree
> Into a Merry Pond, which under them doth lye,
> Waxe ripe, and taking wing, away in flockes doe flye.

He could have read about them not only in Gerald, but also
in Giraldus. The Welshman, who saw them in Ireland,
says that bishops and men of religion do not scruple to eat
these barnacle geese on fasting days, arguing that born of
trees, not of eggs, they are not flesh. He points out, however, that if anyone had eaten of the thigh of Adam, who
was not born of flesh, he would not be guiltless of having

eaten flesh.[1] But Drayton would not have been interested in casuistry, his main interest being mythology; he might have said with Tibullus *"rura cano rurisque deos."*

The mythology is of the poet's own making, natural objects personified. Sometimes it is connected with classical mythology; Albion, who according to Milton ruled the land for forty-four years,[2] was Neptune's son. The land itself could hardly be personified, but Albion, a giant, was its Genius. Islands with their separate individuality are easily turned into persons; even in maps they look like children, the land's offspring; Albion begot islands on sea-nymphs to the indignation of their mother, the sea-goddess Amphitrite. Three of his children lie in Poole harbour, Brownsea, Furzey and little Helen; the harbour was at one time a bay, but Albion drew its ends close together, so protecting the children from the wrath of their grandmother. Better known are his three children in the Thames estuary, Sheppey, Grain and Canvey; before crossing over to Gaul, where he was slain by Hercules, Albion entrusted them to the tuition of their grandfather Neptune. An island that might have benefited by such tuition is Lundy in the Bristol Channel,

> A lustie black-brow'd Girle, with forehead broad and hie
> Who often hath bewitcht the Sea-gods with her eye.

Mountains and hills are not difficult to personify; yet Snowdon, several mountains in one, might present a problem;

> O what a monster had in man been seen
> Had every thumb and toe a mountain been![3]

Drayton's usual method is to move them to make a speech.

[1] *Itinerary of Ireland.*   [2] *The History of England.*   [3] Traherne.

Neighbouring mountains would hardly approve of Skid-daw's proud speech:

> Great Hills farre under me, but as my Pages lye;
> And when my Helme of Clouds upon my head I take
> At very sight thereof, immediately I make
> Th' Inhabitants about, tempestuous stormes to feare.

But little Stiperstones makes a speech the neighbouring hills commend by holding up their hands. Rivers with their movement and sound are readily turned to live beings. Drayton personifies them, though not with the art of Ovid who tells how the Hebrus and other rivers, lamenting the death of Orpheus, were swollen with their own tears, and the Nile was so fired by love of Euanthe that all his mighty water could not quench the flame. Ever since Alpheus pursued the nymph Arethusa rivers have been lovers. A large part of *Poly-Olbion* is taken up with their love affairs, the most notable that of the Thames.

The lovely Isis, Cotswold's heir, was wooed and won by Tame, old Chiltern's son; their union resulted in a child, begotten, born and bred in the same moment, the famous Thames.

> They send him to the Court of great *Oceanus*,
> The Worlds huge wealth to see; yet with a full intent,
> To wooe the lovely Nymph, faire *Medway*, as he went.

But on his way he fell in love with a Surrey nymph, whom he met opposite Hampton Court. His parents heard with dismay of how he loitered and wound about in his course. Meanwhile the nymph's mother had taken alarm and gave her warning; but the warning the nymph treated

> as vain and idle dreames,
> Compar'd with that high joy, to be belov'd of Tame.

Determined to put a stop to their meeting, the mother raised difficulties in the form of hills, but the nymph, working day and night, bored her way beneath them for three miles. Yet all she gained was the name Mole. Compelled to continue on his course, Thames passed London, "lying like a halfe Moon," and was joined in wedlock to Medway. Unfortunately,

> Although with *Medway* matcht, he never could remove
> The often quickning sparks of his more ancient love;

and with each incoming tide he steals his way back towards Hampton Court. But he never gets beyond Teddington! The Thames is of all rivers the most fatuous.

Montgomery Castle

STEPPING off the bus, I ran for shelter to the door of the town hall. The rain fell, not in drops, but in long slanting lines, striking the market square in white splashes that had the appearance of snow. Such a lashing seemed unkind to Montgomery, perhaps the most dignified small town in Britain. Indistinct at first, buildings loomed out of the wet haze, and out of my memory. But I had come to see the Castle, and as the rain slackened, I took the road, now a shallow water-course, that steeply climbs the Castle Hill. It was strange to pass The Dragon, where I had eaten and slept, unrecognised by that watchful monster. When the Castle, standing on its lofty mound, suddenly emerged from a mist, it looked tall and impressive; but closer acquaintance reduced it to meaningless masonry that hardly deserved to be called a ruin. But if the mist had magnified the Castle, it sadly diminished the view, twenty miles contracted to twenty yards. And what it disclosed was not cheerful, half-naked trees and long grasses depressed by rain. But what I was seeing that autumn day was primroses.

They were the primroses John Donne saw, riding up the hill one April evening; "Primrose hill" he calls it. As they shone in the dusk, he may have thought,

> their infinitie
> Make a terrestriall Galaxie,
> As the small starres doe in the skie.

But he had had a tiring ride from Polesworth in Warwickshire, his mind occupied with a poem, *Goodfriday, 1613. Riding Westward*; also he was looking forward to a long talk with Magdalen; he would think no more of primroses that evening unless it occurred to him that next day he might present them to Magdalen, not in a bouquet, but in a poem. He had presented her with the *Holy Hymns and Sonets*, of which Isaak Walton, regretting their loss, says, "doubtless they were such, as they two now sing in heaven." He had written *The Relique*, foretelling that if his grave should be broken up to entertain a second guest, the gravedigger would spy

> A bracelet of bright haire about the bone;

that, too, he may have presented, for he had introduced into it, though indirectly, the name Magdalen. That evening the primroses may have offered themselves as the subject of a poem on the morrow.

The Primrose, being at Montgomery Castle, upon the hill might be called a flower-study, having, in fact, a somewhat studied look.

> I walke to finde a true Love; and I see
> That 'tis not a mere woman, that is shee,
> But must, or more, or lesse than woman bee.

The more or less will depend on what he finds; a primrose with six petals will betoken a Love who is more than woman, an object of Platonic adoration; a primrose with four a Love who is less, which would be nothing at all.

> Yet know I not, which flower
> I wish; a sixe, or foure.

Happily he finds neither, only the five, which betokens that his Love is perfect woman.

Live Primrose then, and thrive
With thy true number five.

But unfortunately it occurs to Donne that digits are either even or odd, and five, first number to include the even in two and the odd in three, is an all-inclusive number! It betokens a Love that would so absorb him that he would be less than man. Every primrose tells the same tale: "women may take us all." One wonders what Magdalen thought of the poem; perhaps she said, "How like Jack."

Riding Westward is called in one of the manuscripts *Riding to Sir Edward Herbert in Wales*; and as we know that Magdalen's son, a much travelled man, was in England at the time, we may suppose he was at Montgomery Castle that Good Friday evening to welcome his old friend, Jack Donne. One who in those days could write his *Autobiography* had a sense of his own importance, and perhaps he did most of the talking. If it was of himself he talked, he had a remarkable subject. Ben Jonson could address him:

If men get name, for some one virtue: Then
What man art thou, that art so many men,
All-vertuous HERBERT! on whose every part
Truth might spend all her voyce, *Fame* all her art.

Even his person was remarkable; when he was in middle age, he grew three inches in height; he weighed more than men taller and fatter than himself; he had a pulse on the top of his head. There were other remarkable things about him, as he hints, but he mentions only his good looks. When as a young man he was presented to Queen Elizabeth, she patted him on the head and said it was a pity he had married so early; it was at the age of fifteen. There were few things, at least suitable for a gentleman, in which he was not accomplished; in singing and lute-playing he excelled. He was a good swordsman: "I think I shall not speak vaingloriously of myself, if I say, that no man understood the use of his weapon better than I did." He handed out challenges to a duel as though they were invitations to dinner; yet he does not appear to have fought a duel. It was by his pen, not his sword, that he most distinguished himself; *De Veritate*, the first book of metaphysics to be written in England, made the name Lord Herbert of Cherbury widely known throughout Europe. To his friends, however, he would be best known, not as a metaphysician, but as a metaphysical poet.

Probably Lord Herbert is one of the poets ridiculed by Davenant in *The Platonick Lovers*. Though they write of Platonic love, they have nothing to do with Plato:

> They father on him a fantastic love
> He never knew, poor gentleman.

Plato was so far from being a Platonic lover himself that a character in the play knows the very house in Athens, he thinks it was a haberdasher's, where the philosopher kept a wench. None the less Lord Herbert was a Platonist. For Socrates in the *Phaedrus* all beauty we perceive is derivative; in seeing it, we are transported with the recollection of the true Beauty. So it is for Lord Herbert:

> All Beauties vulgar eyes on earth do see,
> At best but some imperfect Copies be,
> Of those the Heavens did at first decree.

As it was in human beauties Socrates saw the Copie, he is not far from Platonism in saying in a *Ditty*,

> Now that the *April* of your youth adorns
> The Garden of your face.

To some beauties, however, he appears to have been

indifferent, though they must have been familiar. "I conceive it a fine study, and worthy of a gentleman to be a good botanic." Probably he was a good botanic, for Thomas Johnson on his famous botanical tour, the first to be made and described in Britain, was entertained by him at Montgomery Castle. No doubt he made tours himself, but as he was accompanied by a servant carrying "icones," pictures copied from herbals as a means of identifying plants, they would be mostly short tours in the country surrounding the Castle. For its plants he may have had sharp eyes, but so far as its Beauties were concerned he must have suffered from a black-out. For he had an adoration of black; it subdues all colours, and is neither changed by day nor hid by night; only our own darkness makes us think it dark;

> Blackness is a spark
> Of light inaccessible.

But that surrounding country! It is a borderland, where those old enemies, Wales and England, meet in the friendliest fashion, like Homeric heroes, Trojan and Greek, embracing each other and exchanging gifts. Nowhere else do bare hills and rich valleys agree so pleasantly to differ. Both countries contributing their best, a Montgomery man or a Shropshire lad might go so far as to say it was the most charming part of Britain. On that foggy afternoon on Castle Hill I could not have gone so far; perhaps I never could, halted by the Tweed.

The Swan of Usk

IF Henry Vaughan, in calling his book *Olor Iscanus*, implied that he was the Swan of Usk, it was an odd name for a poet. Swans do not sing; Coleridge is not serious when he says,

> Swans sing before they die,

though no doubt he is when he adds,

>   'twere no bad thing
> Did certain persons die before they sing.

Perhaps it was for her looks rather than her verses that Anna Seward was called Swan of Lichfield. Vaughan may have remembered that swans frequently sing in the Roman poets, of whom he was a great reader; but they are dying swans that sing, and all his poems were written long before his death. Portia could not have said of him as of Bassanio,

>   he makes a swan-like end,
> Fading in music.

Otherwise Swan of Usk is not an unsuitable name for Vaughan. He lived almost all his life close to the river, an unremarkable life except for his marrying his deceased wife's sister. And as in travelling along its wide valley we get glimpses of the river, so we do in reading his poems, unusual glimpses at times, as when we see it in winter

>   slowly float
> All bound up in an Icie Coat.

He hoped to be the river's poet, even as holy Orpheus was poet of the headlong Hebrus. (A strange hope, for the headlong river swept away the poet's head.) And he would make it famous:

> I'le leave behind me a *large, kind* light,
> As shall *redeem* thee from *oblivious night.*

The image of light shining in darkness is characteristic of Vaughan, and for a white light he had a peculiar feeling. It might have been a reason for calling himself Swan of Usk.

But perhaps it was only to the book he gave the name, and his friends, Aubrey and Anthony Wood, transferred it to the poet; as its author he had another name for himself, Mr Henry Vaughan *Silurist.* He lived in a part of Wales occupied in the time of Tacitus by a tribe, the Silures, and that he called himself Silurist suggests it was a country of which he was proud. When he says,

> If *Eden* be on earth at all
> 'Tis that, which we the *Country* call,

it is no doubt particularly to Brecknockshire he refers. It is a land rich in trees and streams,

> *Hony* in Woods, *Juleps* in Brooks;

but the Usk is the making of it. Perhaps that river has not the distinction of the Wye or the even finer Upper Towy, but it flows through a valley which "may vie with all others in Wales for extent of beauty, and is, perhaps, nowhere so much diversified as between Brecknock and Abergavenny." What Giraldus Cambrensis found pleasant in that part of the valley would be its rich vegetation. There Nature is proud of herself, making a lavish display of her wealth, yet at the same time, as though wealth were not all, disclosing ascetic heights in the bare Brecon

Beacons. These mountains have a lonely look; though they are the nearest mountains to London, one has the feeling they are seldom trod.

The Beacons do not come into Vaughan's poems, though they may have been the home of the eagle that flew as fast

As if his *Wings* contended with his sight.

Mountains in his age were not admired; for Andrew Marvell they deformed the earth and frightened heaven. As a country doctor visiting patients in high remote farms Vaughan may not even have appreciated hills; perhaps he felt like Defoe: "the *English* jestingly (and I think not improperly) call it *Breakneckshire*: 'Tis Mountainous to an Extremity." But to the valley itself he responds in his poems; it is as though it poured into them some of its wealth:

The unthrift Sunne shot vitall gold
A thousand peeces.

Its prevailing green is vivid, Irish-like, and after white green was his favourite colour. Both colours had a spiritual value, and the valley's spring meadows and blossoming trees may have suggested the heavenly scene,

A fresh, immortal *green* there dwells,
And spotless *white* is all the wear.
Dear, secret *Greenness*!

Valley and poet show the same quick transitions of mood, the sunlit valley darkened by a sudden cloud-shadow, the poet, his head crown'd with roses, meeting with a dead man.

Vaughan was not a descriptive poet, at least not of places. Llangorse Lake, the second largest natural sheet of water in Wales, lay a mile or so from his home; it is the scene of a poem by the famous Dafydd ap Gwilym in which he calls

a swan's long neck its fishing-rod, but a "drousie Lake",
it woke little interest in Vaughan. The Ffrwdgrech Falls,
if they are *The Water-fall* of the poem, were an exception.
Often on his way back from visiting a patient he may have
stopped on the bridge and, hitching his horse to a tree,
have scrambled down the bank. He almost tells us so:

> Dear stream! dear bank, where often I
> Have sate, and pleas'd my pensive eye.

His eye was pensive; he thought through his senses, his
eye teaching him to read in the waterfall

> What sublime truths, and wholesome themes,

and his ear to transpose its sound into sonorous verse with
a marvellous correspondence:

> With what deep murmurs through time's silent stealth,
> Doth thy transparent, cool and watry wealth
> > Here flowing fall,
> > And chide, and call,
> As if his liquid, loose Retinue staid
> Lingring, and were of this steep place afraid.

The poem falls away after its opening like the river after
the waterfall. That sometimes happens in Vaughan's poems,
and need not be regarded as a fault. Welsh poets may not
aim at organic progression in the English mode; they may
be content with local effects. And he is at one with them in
the way he sometimes packs image with image, as in
Son-dayes:

> The Creatures *Jubile*; Gods parle with dust;
> Heaven here; Man on those hills of Myrrh, and floures;
> Angels descending; the Returns of Trust;
> A Gleame of glory, after six-days-shoures.

That the passage reminds us of George Herbert is not

surprising; he, too, was a Welshman. After all, it may be just fancy to see in Vaughan's poems a response to the Usk Valley. Gold and white and green are much affected by Welsh poets as significant colours. And it is suggestive that Vaughan uses the word "white" in the same wide sense as they use the corresponding Welsh word; it may, for example, mean holy, as in "a white, Celestiall thought." And they also have quick transitions of mood; two moods may even coincide, as in Llywelyn Goch's warm, cold feeling at the grave of his love, "Come up, thou of the foxglove cheeks, from thy sad bed of clay."

It is characteristic of Welsh poets to put things in a way that seems casual, yet is startling. Aneirin, in describing a battle, says, "his sword rang in the heads of mothers," and Taliesin sees in a battlefield with its slain "the wide host of England sleep with the light in their eyes." We find the same thing in Vaughan. If he were given to usury, he tells Amoret,

> I should perhaps eate Orphans, and sucke up
> A dozen distrest widowes in one Cup.

He appears to mention, rather than assert, surprising things:

> Yet stones are deep in admiration.

The most remarkable case is in *The World*, a poem which also falls away. How casual, yet startling, is the opening statement,

> I saw Eternity the other night.

Vaughan was Welsh by nature as by birth; he was no more an English poet for writing in English than a Roman for writing in Latin.

There is nothing particularly Welsh in his glorification

of childhood. John Earle was not jesting in his usual fashion when he said of a child: "His soule is yet a white paper unscribled with observations of the world, wherewith at length it becomes a blurr'd Note-booke. The elder hee growes, he is a staire lower from God; and like his first father, much worse in his breeches."[1] Vaughan did not need to be a Welshman to exclaim, as he looked back on his own childhood,

> How brave a prospect is a bright *Back-side*!

Traherne and Wordsworth said much the same thing. What may be Welsh is a warmer feeling for it:

> My dew, my dew! my early love,
> My souls bright food, thy absence kills!

and his desire to return:

> O how I long to travell back
> And tread again that ancient track!

Staying in the same hotel as some Welsh scholars, I put to them the question, "Is Vaughan's poem, *The Retreate*, an example of the Welsh love of returning to the past?" I was thinking of the Eisteddfodau with their Druids, bards and harps, though I might have been thinking of those scholars themselves, for of such Lloyd George said, "When the last truck-load of coal reaches Cardiff, when the last black diamond is dug out of the earth of Glamorgan, there will be men digging gems of pure brilliance from the inexhaustible mines of the literature and language of Wales." One of them, nodding his head significantly, said, "You have something there."

But for Vaughan life was a retreat from his visionary

---

[1] *Micro-cosmographie.*

childhood. That was inevitable, for, as he says in *The Mount of Olives*, "we run all after the present world, and the Primitive Angelical life is quite lost." Yet he looked back on it with a hopeful regret;

> a grief so bright
> 'Twill make the Land of darkness light;
> And while too many sadly roam,
> Shall send me (Swan-like) singing home.

He would be, after all, a dying Swan.

Milton's Pastorals

O NE of Milton's earliest poems begins with the curious invocation, "Hail, Native Language," curious because language is used to invoke Language. After apologising for too great a use of Latin, he points out that while Native Language has a wardrobe full of various attire, he has thoughts that rove about naked. He is clear as to the kind of garment he does not want:

> Not those new fangled toys, and triming slight
> Which takes our late fantasticks with delight.

Evidently the metaphysical poetry of Donne and his friends was popular at Cambridge, but it was not to Milton's taste. He is also clear as to what he does want:

> But cull those richest Robes, and gay'st attire
> Which deepest Spirits, and choicest Wits desire.

From young Milton it is not a surprising request. As a boy of fifteen he had made a paraphrase of Psalm CXXXVI, now well known as the hymn,

> Let us with a gladsome mind;

but he did not refrain from touching up the original, bringing in the Golden-tressed Sun, the horned Moon and her spangled sisters bright. Native Language was wise in not acceding to his boyish request for a rich and gay attire; what he received was country wear, the kind usually called pastoral. Yet it was something he could take a pride in,

for he speaks of twitching his "Mantle blew." He wore it
at Horton, when he was writing his Pastorals, though
when he came to write *Comus*, he added what he calls the
"learned Sock." It is significant that while poets usually
invoke a Muse, Milton invoked Native Language.

When he was invested with his rustic garment is not
certain; he may have worn it at Cambridge, under his
academic gown, as being nearer his heart; there is some
reason for supposing *L'Allegro* and *Il Penseroso* were
written in his university days. Yet Cambridge itself almost
seems ruled out by the insulting remark, "how ill that
place suits the votaries of Apollo!" And he did not like the
Cambridge country; "nor do naked fields please me, where
soft shades are not to be had." But it is clear he enjoyed
the country he wrote about; Dr Johnson said the gaiety of
L'Allegro did not arise from the pleasures of the bottle,
one of the remarks about the Pastorals that made Cowper
want to thrash the old Tory till his pension jingled in his
pocket. The wooded and well-watered Horton country,
lying between the Thames and the Chilterns, might have
inspired him as well as any other to say: "when the air is
calm and pleasant, it were an injury and sullenness against
nature not to go out and see her riches, and partake in her
rejoycing with Heaven and Earth." The enormously fat
elm on Horton's village green suggests a surrounding
richness; so might even the church's grand Norman door
and stout pillars. But whether the Pastorals were written
at Horton or not, its country cannot claim to be their scene;
as they describe no particular season, the Plowman whist-
ling, the Mower whetting his scythe and Thestylis binding
the sheaves, all on one day, so they describe no particular
locality, for none would include a mountain, a castle, a
cathedral and a wide-water'd shore. *Comus* was written at

Horton and performed at Ludlow, but in no dale in
Buckinghamshire or Shropshire grow Musk-roses. At
Horton he also wrote *Lycidas*, and though Aubrey tells us,
"after dinner he used to walke 3 or four houres at a time,"
he never came across

>   desert Caves,
> With wilde Thyme and the gadding Vine o'ergrown,

for Thyme does not grow over caves nor the Vine go
gadding into deserts.

Milton was not a close observer of Nature. Perhaps his
sight was in part to blame. "From twelve years of age, I
hardly ever left my studies, or went to bed before midnight.
This primarily led to my loss of sight." It could not have
improved at Cambridge, or at Horton, where, as he says,
"I spent a complete holiday in pursuing the Greek and
Latin writers." He speaks of dreaming away his time in
the arms of studious retirement, like Endymion with the
moon. His sight must have been poor when he wrote the
Pastorals. If he had been able to distinguish the small low
Knot-grass, he would hardly have said the chewing flocks

> Had ta'en their supper on the savoury Herb;

it would be truer to say that after eating it

> The hungry Sheep look up, and are not fed.

But while poor sight may account for his seeing the Lark,
not a sparrow, bidding him good morrow at his window,
it would not account for his making it do so

>   Through the Sweet-Briar, or the Vine,
>   Or the twisted Eglantine.

The Eglantine is the Sweet-Briar, not twisted like the
Woodbine, but according to other poets and the name's
derivation thorny;

Sweet is the Eglantine, but pricketh near,

his beloved Spenser said. But if his sight was bad, he had
some compensation in his ear for music; the title *L'Allegro*
is suggestive. It was not just Sophocles, but the bird's own
song that inspired the lines,

> And in the violet imbroider'd vale
> Where the love-lorn Nightingale
> Nightly to thee her sad Song mourneth well.

Milton could not hear enough of the Nightingale. Unfortunately he hears too much when in *Paradise Regained*
he makes the bird

> Trill her thick-warbled notes the summer long.

He could not have lived for six years in Horton without
knowing that the bird's song ended in early summer; he
must have been forgetful. No doubt he was also forgetful
when he said a blind Fury slit the thin-spun life of Lycidas;
it should have been a Fate, for a Fury's function was to
punish crime. Certainly he did not intend to give his friend
a bad character.

When Milton was blind, he heard a lady singing finely
and immediately said, "Now, I swear, this lady is handsome." Perhaps he would not have sworn to an inference
drawn from a handsome figure to a fine voice. Sound had a
special significance for him; names with their echoing
associations might mean more to him than their objects.
"Look after the sense, and the sounds will look after
themselves," said Lewis Carroll; when Milton wrote the
passage about the flowers in *Lycidas*, an afterthought and,
as notes show, composed with care, he was looking after
the sounds more than the sense. Gushing brooks and
valleys low are called on

To strew the Laureat Herse where *Lycid* lies.

But the brooks do not respond, and the flowers the valleys strew are not all of a season. The rathe Primrose does not bloom at the same time as the Musk-rose, for "rathe," an uncommon adjective with a common comparative "rather," means early. The Cowslips are wan, though in a previous poem they are yellow, but no doubt they are in half-mourning for Lycidas like the Pansie freakt with jet.

And Daffadillies fill their cups with tears;

but how could that be? Sorrow for Lycidas would not cause them to hold up their down-hanging heads. Milton was writing with his ear rather than with his eye. Poems so written can be strangely affecting. Of a line in *Arcades* A. E. Housman asks, "in these six simple words of Milton—

Nymphs and shepherds, dance no more—

what is it that can draw tears, as I know it can, to the eyes of more readers than one? What in the world is there to cry about?"[1] Whatever it is, it must be more in the sound than in the sense.

Milton's botanical errors are not even peccadilloes; anyone who pointed them out would be trying to show off his knowledge! And it need not amount to much. Nature, usually regarded as feminine, is to be admired by poets rather than investigated, and Milton *sings* her charms. His singing robe fits him to perfection. One might wonder why at the end of *Lycidas* he twitches his "Mantle blew." Perhaps he feels he is outgrowing it.

To morrow to fresh Woods, and Pastures new,

[1] *The Name and Nature of Poetry.*

may be metaphorical language, referring not to future
Pastorals, but to a work he had in mind, "something so
written to after times as they should not willingly let it
die." Whether it would be drama or epic was still uncertain; whichever it was, he would fling off his "Mantle
blew" and Native Language would fit him out in a far
grander style.

Nun-Appleton House

N UN-APPLETON HALL stands a short distance above
the junction of the Wharfe with the Ouse, its front
incorporating a charming portion of the old Nun-Appleton
House, General Fairfax's home. A broad meadow separates
its raised lawn from the river, which here takes a slow
winding course as though unwilling to lose its identity in
the Ouse. In Fairfax's time the meadow could be artificially
flooded; Andrew Marvell describes

> How *Salmons* trespassing are found:
> And Pikes are taken in the Pound.

Whether this was a benefit to the fisher or not, it was to the
farmer, the meadow grass keeping a perennial freshness.
Yet one wonders why the artificial flooding was needed,
for natural floods are so frequent and widespread that the
grass seldom loses its freshness. With trees hanging in
heavy green clouds over the park, the eye receives a sense
of unusual greenness; few visitors to Nun-Appleton Hall
fail to quote the lines,

> Annihilating all that's made
> To a green Thought in a green Shade.

The greenness must have struck Marvell coming from
London; it cannot be by accident that in the small book of
his poems, written mostly at Nun-Appleton but published
after his death, the word "green" occurs twenty-five times.
Green became for him a signal colour;

> No white nor red was ever seen
> So am'rous as this lovely green.

Things of all kinds, almost irrespective of their colour, are
commended as being green; a blossom is green and there
is a green night; the colour so pervades his mind that a
thought can be greener than grass. Strangely enough, he
does not appear to have considered his poems green, as he
did not trouble to have them published. Time has proved
they are evergreen.

General Fairfax did not lose his military interest after
his retirement; he raised an army in the garden of Nun-
Appleton, an army of flowers. Marvell could not have
admired it for its discipline; the bees, who do sentry duty
at night, enter their flowery sentry-boxes only to fall
asleep. But he delighted in the regimental colours:

> See how the Flow'rs, as at Parade,
> Under their *Colours* are displaid:
> Each *Regiment* in order grows,
> That of the Tulip Pinke and Rose.

Yet in *The Mower Against Gardens* it is Marvell himself
who speaks; perhaps he was the Mower, for he could not
have continuously tutored Fairfax's daughter. What he
mainly has against gardens is high cultivation; when
luxurious Man took to pampering his plants as well as
himself,

> The Pink grew then as double as his Mind.

The nature of the duplicity he explains:

> And Flow'rs themselves were taught to paint.

The Mower dislikes painted flowers as Propertius disliked
painted women. His particular dislike is for the streaked
tulip; one of its Onion roots, as he contemptuously calls the

bulbs, was bought for a meadow. The price was not excessive, if, as Lovelace says,

> 'Twas a blithe prince exchanged five hundred crowns
> For a fair turnip;[1]

but to the Mower it seemed excessive; the whole garden was not worth a meadow. It might be adorned with polished statues in the antique style, but, says the Mower, viewing it from a meadow,

> The *Gods* themselves with us do dwell.

Flowers could not have the universal appeal of grass. Beyond the garden is a meadow, and beyond that is grass-land, and more grassland; the whole world is grass! Human beings are tiny creatures in that world:

> And now to the Abbyss I pass
> Of that unfathomable Grass,
> Where Men like Grashoppers appear.

True grasshoppers, being more native to the element, are giants in comparison and can look down on men, can do it in a double sense:

> They, in there squeking Laugh, contemn
> Us as we walk more low than them.

Even mowers, who appear on the scene,

> seem like Israalites to be
> Walking on foot through a green Sea.

But the mowers assert themselves;

> With whistling Sithe, and Elbow strong,
> These Massacre the Grass along.

So grass and men return to their normal size.

[1] *On Sanazar's Being Honoured.*

But trees are also green, and for trees Marvell has as great an affection as for grass, perhaps a greater. To Cowley they seem dull Creatures:

> 'tis not without Cause that she
> Who fled the *God of wit*, was made a tree;[1]

but Marvell puts a different interpretation on the story:

> *Apollo* hunted *Daphne* so,
> Only that She might Laurel grow.

He can turn himself into a tree, becoming identified with the object of his love. Indeed, properly considered, he already is a tree;

> Turn me but, and you shall see
> I was but an inverted Tree.

He is playing with the idea popular with old philosophers, *homo est planta inversa*. Marvell is more original in telling of another transformation:

> Casting the Bodies Vest aside,
> My soul into the boughs does glide.

Ovid changed many people into birds, but never thought of so changing himself. When the soul is in the tree, it is at the height of bliss; yet only of earthly bliss, for it has to prepare itself to be something more, a Bird of Paradise:

> There like a Bird it sits, and sings,
> Then whets, and combs its silver Wings;
> And, till prepar'd for longer flight,
> Waves in its Plumes the various Light.

But many years are to pass before his soul sets out on that longer flight. He will have to play a part in his country's troubled affairs; he hopes it will be an honest

[1] *The Spring.*

E

part, but he can have no idea that he will receive the title "British Aristides." Meanwhile at Nun-Appleton House his country's troubles seem far away:

> How safe, methinks, and strong, behind
> These Trees have I incamp'd my Mind.

But sooner or later he will have to emerge from his shelter.

> Bind me ye *Woodbines* in your 'twines,
> Curle me about ye gadding *Vines*,
> And Oh so close your Circles lace,
> That I may never leave this Place.

Perhaps there is more feeling than we might think in the lines,

> Do you, *O Brambles*, chain me too,
> And courteous *Briars* nail me through.

But while Marvell has this strange affection for grass and trees, he can hardly be placed among the Nature-poets. He can be even critical of Nature; Wordsworth would not have complained that mountains

> The Earth deform and Heaven fright.

And he is not a descriptive poet. He can see things that see him, as, for example, the shining eye of a throstle nesting in a hazel; but his habit is to do natural objects the discredit of regarding them as artificial; woodland trees are "the Columnes of a Temple green," and a wood near a flooded meadow "a green, yet growing Ark." And, after all, his intercourse with Nature lasted only the two years he lived at Nun-Appleton House. Yet Nature in a way meant more to him than to many Nature-poets.

> Fair quiet, have I found thee here,
> And Innocence thy Sister dear!

The peaceful time was the more precious because it would not last. Though his mind

> in the greenness of the Grass
> Did see its hopes as in a Glass,

the Mower cutting down the grass was symbolic. *The Garden* ends significantly with the flower-dial, where

> th'industrious bee
> Computes its time as well as we.

Meanwhile, "easie Philosopher" he can describe himself. Certainly he was an easy philosopher, who could sit in the garden,

> Annihilating all that's made
> To a green Thought in a green Shade.

But a garden is not a grassy meadow, and one might think it could hardly of itself have induced this blissful state of mind. We know that Nun-Appleton House was hospitable: its open door had a portico—the poor, and its rooms a changing furniture—the guests. Aubrey mentions that at times Marvell took wine "to refresh his spirits, and exalt the muse."

Charles Cotton

THE visitor to Alstonefield Church sees an old box-pew with a coat of arms, in which Isaak Walton and Charles Cotton must sometimes have worshipped; a room in Beresford Hall was named Walton's. As they sat side by side, a dove, part of the coat of arms, hung between their heads. It was a fitting symbol of their warm friendship, the more so if it was also symbolic of the river they loved to fish, the Dove.

The friendship between the two seems strange, Walton the elder by thirty-seven years; but his age would have allowed him to make Cotton's acquaintance, for as a friend of his father he would come to know young Charles. But it seems strange in other ways. Walton liked nothing better than to discourse with bishops; Cotton enjoyed gambling with his friends, Lovelace and Suckling. Walton made a small fortune and bought property near his native Stafford; Cotton wasted his patrimony and had to sell his birthplace, Beresford Hall. Walton was a man of simple natural piety, well-named after the meditative patriarch Isaac. As he sits by the Lea, joying in his happy condition, he thankfully remembers what his Saviour said, that the meek shall possess the earth. The quill with which he wrote his *Lives*

Dropped from an Angel's wing.[1]

Cotton wrote *Scarronides*. Some things in that burlesque

[1] Wordsworth, *Sonnet*.

translation of part of the *Aeneid* might have amused
Walton, Cupid called a Tiny, Juno

That scratching, cater-wawling Puss,

god-born Aeneas saying of Venus,

my Mother's a mad Shaver,
No Man alive knows where to have her;

but he would not have approved of what made it perhaps
the most popular poem of its time. We know, however,
nothing against Cotton himself, at least apart from his
wasteful gambling and what we are told of his hiding in a
cave from his duns. Certainly he was loved by his friends;
Lovelace complained of his absence as, he said, the earth
in winter complains of her false lover the sun, making love
to th'antipodes. Cotton says of Walton, "He gives me
leave to call him Father, and I hope is not yet ashamed to
own me for his adopted Son." He can also say, "my father
Walton will be seen twice in no man's company he does not
like." But what more than anything else made them Father
and Son was that they were brothers; each recognised in
the other "a Brother of the Angle."

Both were good anglers, better than Wordsworth if he
had himself in mind when he spoke of a fishing-rod as
"true symbol of hope's foolishness." But the *Compleat
Angler*'s method of angling may seem primitive. Walton's
rod was the butt of some tree, perhaps hazel or willow, six
yards or more in length and thick as a person's arm; from
it hung without a reel a line of twisted horsehair, dyed with
a pint of strong ale and half a pound of soot; at its end was
a baited hook. Plato had a poor opinion of fishermen; in
their method he saw a similarity to the Sophist's; Byron
had the worst opinion of Walton, "this sentimental

savage." For him the *Compleat Angler* with its poetic
description and quietude had no charm;

> Whatever Isaac Walton sings or says,
> The quaint, old, cruel coxcomb, in his gullet
> Should have a hook, and a small trout to pull it.

Yet it could not have occurred to Walton that he was
torturing the creatures, grasshopper, beetle, worm, even
frog, that he used as live bait. "I am not of a cruel nature,
I love to kill nothing but fish." Yet when he and Venator
came on the otter's cubs, "Here are her young ones, no
less than five," he said; "come let's kill them all." Otters
were "villanous vermin," for like himself they caught fish.
Artificial flies had long been in use, the method of making
them described in the early *Treatyse of Fysshynge wyth an
Angle*; but their use seems to have been restricted. Dame
Juliana Berners, or whoever wrote the *Treatyse*, explains
that it is printed along with other works to make it too
expensive to be bought by "ydle persones," the common
people. Angling with artificial flies was suitable for a fine
gentleman like Charles Cotton, not for a London iron-
monger like Isaak Walton. Cotton's skill in the art led to
his writing an account of it, which was added to the fifth
edition of Walton's work. Written in fourteen days, it
completed the *Compleat Angler*.

Cotton tries to carry on Walton's descriptive manner,
but the scene is greatly changed. Walton fished by the Lea,
which flows through Charles Lamb's "hearty, homely,
loving Hertfordshire"; Cotton fishes by the Dove, which
seeks in Beresford Dale a shelter from high exposed hills.
"I entered the Peak, a country beyond comparison uglier
than any other I have seen in England"; Gray might
hardly have modified the words in writing to Wharton of

the Low Peak. If it was his Hertfordshire Edward Young
had in mind when he said,

> Green fields, and shady groves, and crystal springs,
> And larks, and nightingales, are odious things,[1]

one wonders what he would have said of the Cotton
country. Cotton makes the most of it; in fact, he makes
more. "Bless me, what mountains are here!" Viator ex-
claims. "Are we not in Wales?" He is in dread of falling
over a precipice, and surprised to see a church. The bridge
across the Dove, still called Viator's, was not two fingers
broad; a mouse could hardly have gone over it. Altogether
it was an ill Landskip. Compared with the soft South it
had a severe appearance; so at least must have thought Sir
Thomas Browne, or Tom, as he was when he wrote home
to his father: "If I had been of Darbishiere I should never
have doubted the truth of Ovid's story, that wee were all
produc'd of stones." Cotton, returning from the South,
found himself

> The same dull Northern clod I was before;

when his return happened to be in winter,

> Each Hair was frozen to an Icicle.

But the Fishing-house still stood firm and faithful in the
selfsame place;

> I left it four months since, and ten to one
> I goe a-fishing e'er two days are gone.

For Walton angling and poetry went together; they
were so much one that Piscator in the *Incomplete Angler*
asserts that a proficient can catch a fish with a fine line of

[1] *Satire V.*

poetry, provided he lets it fall with bated breath.[1] Cotton's part of the *Compleat Angler*, having no poetry, hardly seems part of the *Compleat Angler*. But no doubt when the friends went fishing together, they read and recited poems. Walton would read from his favourite Du Bartas, perhaps the passage about the strange fish, the adulterous sargus, that taking to land,

> Goes courting she-goats on the grassy shore,
> Horning their husbands that had horns before.

Cotton could have quoted the more remarkable case of the Buxton Naiad, who nurses two neighbouring springs, one hot and the other cold; it is one of the *Wonders of the Peak* that this Naiad

> Should have her Silver Breasts at once to flow,
> One with *warm Milk*, t'other with *melted Snow*.

What is more probable is that, sitting by the Dove, he read to his friend *Stanzes Irreguliers*, for the poem celebrates Beresford Dale and is dedicated to Mr Izaak Walton. As he thinks of the wild surrounding country (if not so wild now, still with a commanding beauty), he wonders what instigated Providence

> to damn me to a Place,
> Where Nature's only in disgrace.

But his home was in Beresford Dale! where he would, as he says,

> Contented live, and there contented die.

Anglers have not improved the Dove, which now runs between formal banks and is crossed by frequent water-breaks; it has a mere prettiness, on which the dark over-

[1] F. C. Burnand.

hanging cliffs look down with a frown. It must have been more of a Nymph in Cotton's time:

> Oh my beloved Nymph! fair Dove.

He even goes on, "Oh my beloved Rocks!" "Oh my beloved Caves!"

> Good God! how sweet are all things here!

Henry Vaughan, addressing the Usk, says that poets who have sat and sung by rivers become in time their genii, and it is believed

> that from this sickly air
> They pass to regions more refin'd and fair.

No doubt Isaak Walton and Charles Cotton are now such genii, one of the Lea, the other of the Dove, and are in those meadows,

> Where all in white they walk, discourse, and sing.

But it is doubtful if they still angle; Ovid tells us that fish swam unharmed in the reign of Saturn, that Golden Age.

Edmund Waller

O N Edmund Waller's ornate tomb in Beaconsfield churchyard Mr Rymer, the Historiographer Royal, inscribed, *inter poetas sui temporis facile princeps.* But perhaps Waller was better known as a politician and wit than as a poet. His political career was remarkable. Probably no one else entered Parliament so young and so old; at the age of sixteen he was elected member for Amersham, and at the age of eighty for Saltash in Cornwall. And there was the Waller Plot. That brought him into disgrace, but he lived in an age of sudden and great changes, when things could be conveniently forgotten. Back in Parliament, he was "the delight of the house." No one could keep up a grudge against a man of his wit; Charles II smiled at his excuse for *Upon His Majesty's happy return* being a poorer poem than *A Panegyric to my Lord Protector*: "Poets, sir, succeed better in fiction than in truth." His wit even overcame the social disadvantage of what Dr Johnson calls his "obstinate sobriety"; and the Doctor quotes the case of a Mr Savile who said, "No man in England should keep him company without drinking but Ned Waller." Yet it was not just of a witty teetotaller that Burke said, "'tis surprising so much softness and so much grandeur could dwell in one soul." Perhaps he saw the softness in Waller's sympathy with persecuted sects, shown, for example, in his defence of Quakers: "These people are like children's tops, whip them and they stand up, let them alone and they fall."

The grandeur he must have thought he saw in Waller's poetry.

Inter poetas sui temporis facile princeps! Milton was of that age, but Mr Rymer may have shared Waller's opinion that *Paradise Lost* was remarkable for nothing but its length. In any case "easily the best poet of his age" was probably how most of his contemporaries regarded Waller. "Nothing in our age is more preposterous than the running judgments upon poets and poetry":[1] what was true of Ben Jonson's age was no doubt true of Waller's age, and, indeed, of most others. Judgments are particularly affected by what Shakespeare calls the one touch of nature that makes the whole world kin, the love of novelty. To his contemporaries Waller's verse was something new; how smoothly it flowed through the polished couplets! They were carried away by it. So we might gather from an *Introduction to Waller's Poems*: "He was indeed the priest of English Verse. The Tongue came into his Hands like a rough diamond: He polished it first, and to that degree, that all artists since him have admired the Workmanship, without pretending to mend it." Young Waller himself was conscious of his priestly mission. "When he was a brisque young sparke, and first studyed poetry, 'Methought,' said he, 'I never saw a good copie of English verses; they want smoothness; then I began to essay.'"[2]

"Walking in his fine woods, the poetique spirit came upon him."[3] We can believe it came on him in those Chiltern woods, in autumn when the beeches kindle their bonfires without waiting for the Fifth of November, and even in winter when they stand in a thin blue haze that in spring will turn to bluebells. His smooth persuasive verse

[1] Ben Jonson, *Timber: or, Discoveries.*
[2] Aubrey, *Brief Lives.*   [3] Ibid.

inclines us to believe more, that he became a second
Orpheus, casting a spell over animals and trees.

> While in the park I sing, the listening deer
> Attend my passion, and forget to fear:
> When to the beeches I report my flame,
> They bow their heads, as if they felt the same.

For smoothness of verse helps wit, making strange things
seem credible; words slipping off the tongue, wild state-
ments are easily swallowed. When Donne calls harshly to
the sun, "Sawcy pedantique wretch," it pays no attention;
but when Waller addresses it in his suave manner,

> Stay, Phoebus! stay;
> The world to which you fly so fast,
> Conveying day
> From us to them—

it stops to listen before flying off to America. Sacharissa
could easily have believed that what poets usually speak of
as a flame was in Waller's case a conflagration; there was
no need for him to instruct the trees:

> Ye lofty beeches, tell this matchless dame,
> That if together ye fed all one flame,
> It would not equalize the hundredth part
> Of what her eyes have kindled in my heart.

The lovely Amoret, troubled to think what she looked like
in her illness, must have been comforted to hear,

> And as pale sickness does invade
> Your frailer part, the breaches made
> In that frail lodging, still more clear
> Make the bright guest, your soul, appear.

She would have been the more gratified as the rest of the

poem does not suggest she was an ascetic saint. Strangely enough, the image of the soul and its lodging reappears in a very different poem, the last he wrote, or rather dictated, for well over eighty he could neither read nor write:

> The soul's dark cottage, battered and decayed,
> Lets in new light through chinks that time has made;
> Stronger by weakness, wiser men become,
> As they draw near to their eternal home.

Thomas Ellwood the Quaker, visiting his "courteous friend," read the poem to him in his last illness. If he remembered the Amoret poem, he must have felt with Burke, "What shadows we are, and what shadows we pursue."

Rutland

PERHAPS it is partly because of its smallness that we
have a peculiar affection for Rutland. "Indeed it is but
a pestle of a lark," says Fuller, a lark's leg being proverbial
of something tiny. As though from a sense of modesty it
does not claim to be a shire like its neighbours, its name
being plain Rutland. It may be difficult to find on a map
unless we look for Stamford, of which it owns a fragment.
And most things in Rutland are on a small scale, hills and
rivers, villages and the county town, Oakham; many of its
churches have bellcotes instead of towers, reminding us of
small churches in wild Wales. The turf-maze at Wing, one
of the last left in England, seems suited to those small
people, the fairies; we might safely say with Alonso in
The Tempest,

> This is as strange a maze as e'er men trod;
> And there is in this business more than nature
> Was ever conduct of.

It seems appropriate that this county should have produced
Geoffrey Hudson. When the Duchess of Buckingham entertained Charles I and his Queen at Burley-on-the-Hill, a
large cold pie was laid on the table, and out of it, when the
crust was broken, stepped Master Geoffrey. Better than
Shakespeare's Clown he could have said,

> When that I was a little tiny boy.

He grew up to be the smallest Englishman. Fuller remarks on the congruity, "the least man of the least county."

But there is a sense in which Rutland overflows its boundary, for the Ketton stone, almost as famous as the Barnack, was extensively used throughout the country. A poor oolite, it has shown a Christian virtue in making many rich. Pale yellow, but weathering to grey as though in sympathy with a building's age, it is one of those stones which have helped to carry on a fine architectural tradition. Because it has been the making of Stamford in a literal sense, it has also been the making of it in a figurative, for Stamford comes near being the most attractive town in England. It has been used in so many buildings scattered about the country, cathedrals, colleges, manor-houses, that it might be said that Rutland, the smallest English county, is also the most extensive.

But perhaps in our affection for Rutland we are reciprocating its friendliness. Among themselves, at least, the people appear to be remarkably social; they are so neighbourly that you seldom see an isolated cottage; even the farm-houses are usually in a village. And there is a large number of those buildings which, though poor places, are part of England's architectural wealth, alms-houses; they must have been charitable wool merchants who sent their wares down the Welland on the way to Calais. Another amiable feature of the county is the number of dovecotes or pigeon-houses; Belmesthorpe has two, one of them occupied, not by pigeons, but by people. These birds were always regarded as symbolic of affection. Mercutio points out to Romeo that "dove" rhymes with "love," and even in Chaucer's time the words were synonymous; Ianuarie's wife was "douve swete with eyen columbyne." As each dovecote has a hundred times as many pigeon-holes as a desk, the country must have swarmed with these amorous birds. They are mostly gone now, their houses filled with farmers' implements; but how loving a county it must have been when they strutted on every roof, cooing and billing in the sun!

The stranger may feel that Rutland's friendliness is extended to himself, for footpaths are common, inviting him to cross fields, and almost every road offers him a seat. By nature the country is cold, much of it lying high, exposed to chill winds which blow over the Lincolnshire fens; but the soil is mostly of a warm welcoming red. It is not the crude Devon red, but it is red enough to have given rise to the idea that Rutland means Red Land, while it means Rota's Land; in one place it was red enough to make me imagine a group of mole-hills in a field were hens, Rhode Island Reds. But this small county is more than friendly; its lonely roads give a sense of intimacy; yet they are strangely silent, as though leaving the land to speak.

Rutland, of course, is among the fox-hunting shires. That should not prejudice us against it if what I was told one night in an inn is true, the fox *likes* to be hunted. How full of envy must have been the Rutland fox that, seated on a railway line, watched so intently another fox being chased by the hounds, that a passing train cut off his brush! But a fox-hunting county with its manor-houses and parks might be thought to have an exclusive air, yet, judging by the horseshoes hung in the Hall of Oakham Castle, it is the most hospitable county in England. No other county has anything of the kind to show. They are the gifts of visitors, for each peer of the realm who entered the town presented a horseshoe to the market-clerk, or else a sum of money which went to the making of a model. As some of the models are enormous, the place has the look of a celestial smithy, or perhaps an infernal one for those who have to make a forced appearance at the assizes or quarter-sessions. They hang in the old natural way, the ends pointing down, not according to the modern superstition that, forming a hollow, they keep in the luck. Formerly they hung outside, and they might be better there still, if they distract our eyes from the beauty of the Hall itself, particularly of its foliated capitals, a unique work of the late twelfth century.

Rutland may be felt as friendly in another way: it has much that is attractive and, unlike Northamptonshire, almost nothing that is repellent. Its neighbour is famous for fine churches, but Rutland, though with little fame, has them in as high a proportion. The most remarkable is the little Norman church of Tickencote. It lies in a pleasant hollow below the Great North Road, and, though the traffic roars overhead, it gives the impression of being asleep. Outside, its aged appearance makes you feel other churches are upstarts; inside, the chancel arch looks as if it had been bent out of shape by the weight of years, though the cause may have been a settlement of the ground. Perhaps it is too somnolent or too old to give the welcome other things in Rutland give to strangers; for when you enter, faces on corbels, showing their teeth or shooting out the tongue, grin at you, an ephemeral creature.

Rutland itself has an attractive character; we feel it even in the lie of the land. It does not stretch away from us in level plains like its neighbours, Lincolnshire and Northamptonshire; it discloses itself in shallow valleys and rises to face us in low hills. As all is in small compass and irregular, scenes quickly change; yet they are more or less true to type. From an upland we look down on a broad valley, broken by a brook as alive as its wind-blown willows; beyond it the eye rises to an expansive slope dotted with

F

tiny hamlets and tree-clumps, which, if respectively put together, would make a village and a wood. The pedestrian appreciates these variations on a theme, while the motorist may be conscious of nothing more than a petty charm. On him, as he casually hastens through it, this undulating land may have an odd way of taking its revenge. So I felt one evening, when, motoring in the Ryhall district, I received a shock. As the car descended into a valley, the sun suddenly sank; as it climbed out of it, the sun as suddenly rose. Sunset and sunrise followed so fast that several days were gone in a few minutes. Tickencote had made me feel I was an ephemeral creature, but that was only an intimation of mortality; this experience of fleeting days was the real thing!

Rockroses

My feeling for Rockroses goes back to my Edinburgh school-days, though days spent in playing truant on Arthur's Seat, where the plant was plentiful, should hardly be called school-days. Certainly they were sunny days, for the Rockrose, a Helianthemum, Flower of the Sun, closes to a cloudy sky. That so small a plant should be called a Rose is a tribute to its charm, and of this charm it appears to be well aware itself, for like a true Rose it is so sure of attracting insects that it offers no honey. Perhaps I picked the plant, but it was only to see how, indignant at being picked, it almost immediately dropped its petals. It was of course the Common Rockrose I saw on Arthur's Seat. Long afterwards I was to see its rare relation, White Rockrose; that was on Brean Down near Weston-super-Mare, where I was trespassing, a milder form of pleasure than playing truant.

Two other Rockroses then remained for me to see, the Hoary and the Spotted. They grow in North Wales, though the Spotted, by its wiry, almost shrublike growth, suggests it has travelled from an earlier home, the warm limestone rocks of the Mediterranean. It was fortunate I knew places where they grew, not just the general locality, but the particular spots to within yards. Yet it was also unfortunate. The search for a plant should begin with hope, and this hope should gradually sink till it is almost submerged in despair; then should come the joyful moment when we suddenly recognise what we never saw before. The plant may be a poor thing, but it outshines Paestan Roses. But for these two rare Rockroses I should not even need to search; it made them seem common.

The Hoary, the less rare, grows on the top of a hill in Anglesey; "there the reverend *Hugh Davies* pointed it out to me," said Pennant nearly two centuries ago. The hill looks towards the island that with its ancient hermit's oratory is called Priestholme, but is also named after its present occupants Puffin Island. It stands in a country of undulating hillocks, rich with golden gorse, yet with naked rock showing through the tattered turf. These hillocks, with the small fields, lanes and tiny streams, wake in the pedestrian a friendly, even intimate feeling. But I had no such feeling the day I set out to find the plant and could not even find the hill. The undulating hillocks were continually rising up to obstruct my view. And no one I questioned seemed to have heard of the hill; yet it was a well-known hill, noted for its prehistoric camp and much frequented by picnickers. When children in a school playground all shook their heads, I felt almost indignant. How could they not know of a hill only a mile or so away? At last, with the hope of obtaining a wider prospect, I climbed some exposed rocks. I gazed all around, but saw nothing resembling a hill. I was not alone; there was a courting couple, who fell apart as I approached and asked, "Do you know of a hill called Arthur's Seat?" "If you mean Arthur's Table, you are standing on it," the young man said. I grasped the truth; so familiar with Arthur's Seat near Edinburgh, I had been mistranslating the Welsh name, Bwrdd Arthur. They were a pleasant couple, who pretended to be greatly interested when I showed them the Hoary Rockrose.

The Spotted Rockrose grows on Holyhead Mountain,

and later in the day, while I was waiting for a bus at
Beaumaris, it was comforting to think that a mountain is a
more conspicuous object than a hill. It was no hardship to
wait at Beaumaris, a town that replacing a marish or salt-
marsh deserves to retain the "Beau." But the journey was
tedious, the Telford road driving straight through the least
attractive part of Anglesey, no abundant cornfields to
explain the name Mother of Wales, no shady oak-groves
to suggest the Druids' college which, as Caesar tells us,
drew students even from Gaul. At Holyhead, a dull town
like most small seaports, I waited for another bus. Though
it was only an hour I waited, while Dean Swift waited
seven days for a boat, I understood his advice: "Whoever
would wish to live long should live here, for a day is longer
than a week, and if the weather be foul, as long as a fortnight."[1] Perhaps I was impatient, for the sky was becoming
somewhat overcast, and I knew, if it became clouded, the
sun-loving plant would close its petals and be difficult to
detect. But that did not happen, and when at length I
stepped off the bus at the mountain, "The weather is
right," I said, "and the season is right," and a little later,
recognising certain landmarks, "the place is right." All
else being right, it was strange one thing should be wrong:
I could not find the Spotted Rockrose.

Next morning at Aber I was still wondering why. Then
something occurred to me which made me leave my breakfast, glance at my watch, reflect a moment and, seizing a
map, hurry from the hotel. I ran across the road and caught
a train. Catching a train is not usually dangerous, but on
this occasion it was, for I literally caught it, the train being
already in motion. At Bangor I changed for Carnarvon,
where I was just in time to miss the Pwllheli bus. I tried to

[1] *Holyhead Journal.*

take a proper interest in the great castle, of which Dr Johnson said, "I did not think there had been such buildings," a remark he might not have made, if those ordered to blow it up had not also been ordered to be economical with the gunpowder. Even in the bus I was restless, grudging the minute or so it stopped at Clynnog Fawr, close to the cruciform church, still as in Leland's time "the fayrest chirch yn al Cairnarvonshire." Yet I felt somewhat ashamed of my impatience, the church reminding me I was on the Saints' Road, of all roads the most sacred. How many had travelled that way, not to return; they left their bones in Bardsey Island, for there surely, where the sun sank, was the Isle of the Blest. Fuller's jest about the twenty thousand was unkind: "it is more facile to find graves in Berdsey for so many saints, than saints for so many graves."[1] Yet even in my chastened mood, induced by thinking of the saints, I yielded to temptation and looked at my watch.

At Pwllheli, boarding a bus for Aberdaron, I took a front seat as though with some idea of getting there sooner. What a fool I was not to be going back to Holyhead Mountain, a much shorter journey. I had taken a dislike to the Mountain; but why? That I failed to find the plant was my own fault. I gave only a grudging interest to the peculiar country I was passing through, the Lleyn. Its bare and yet cultivated appearance made it seem a place apart by more than its remoteness. The landscape was broken by low hills, many of them with curious knobs as though they could be lifted and placed elsewhere; I almost thought they were, for with the sharp bends of the road they took up new and surprising positions. Small fields, green, yellow and brown, lay huddled on their slopes, crushed into

[1] *Worthies of England.*

irregular shapes. The country reminded me of nothing, till, "Why, this is like a Cornish cove," I said, as the bus descended a small rocky ravine to Aberdaron.

Seeking out the local taxi-driver, I was told he was having his dinner. And I had not finished my breakfast. I paced up and down, impatient of the delay, for every minute was precious. When at last he appeared, I explained, showing him a map, that I was in great haste to reach a point along the coast. Though he said nothing, his look was clearly asking, "What is your hurry to go nowhere in particular?" And when, a quarter of an hour later, I sprang from the car and hastened towards the sea-cliff, I felt he followed me with his eyes. Was I going to throw myself over the cliff into the sea? But I stopped short of its edge and paced about with bent head, pondering deeply before I took the fatal leap. Then I acted wisely, flinging myself down on my knees in prayer. The occasion was suitable for prayer in a way, for what I knelt beside was a dying flower. It dropped first one petal, then another, then two together and then the last. But it was a happy ending; the flower had had a long life, at least an hour longer than the usual span of Spotted Rockroses. Their peculiarity is to fall away about noon, when the plants become difficult to detect. What I had forgotten at Holyhead Mountain I remembered at Aber.

The Leasowes

IN the season of 1762 Shenstone's visitors included one
Duke and his Duchess, three Earls, eight Lords and
seven Ladies, one Marquis, one Baron and, even more
distinguished, Mrs Montague and Mr Pepys. So we gather
from a letter to his friend, Richard Graves, and though he
expresses himself modestly, it must have been gratifying
to one who thought, "A Coach with a Coronet is a pretty
kind of Phoenomenon at my Door—Few things prettier."
Of course he was accustomed to crowds of visitors of a
different class; to his friend, Richard Jago, he writes, "It
is now Sunday evening, and I have been exhibiting myself
in my walks to no less than a hundred and fifty people, and
with no less state and vanity than a Turk in his seraglio."
Yet it was not so much to see him his visitors came as to
view his farm, The Leasowes.

The farm-house looked down on Halesowen, now a
Worcestershire town, but at the time in a detached part of
Shropshire, Admir'd SALOPIA. The name, Leasowes,
means Grazing Farm, and there were cows, said to have
been selected by Shenstone for the pattern on their hides;
sheep also—

> My hills are white-over with sheep,

he says; he tells, too, that he fed Poultry, Ducks, Pigeons,
Swans. The land being hilly and including two small
wooded dingles, he saw the possibilities of the place, all

that a farm might be. "Fields of Corn make a pleasant
Prospect, and if the Walks were a little taken care of that
lie between them, if the natural Embroidery of the Meadows
were helpt and improved by some small Additions of Art,
and the several Rows of Hedges set off by Trees and
Flowers, that the Soil was capable of receiving, a man
might make a pretty Landskip of his own Possessions."
The result was the *Ferme Ornée*, Ornamented Farm, which
drew distinguished visitors from all parts of the country.
Dr Johnson, not an admirer of Shenstone, had to admit
that "he made his little domain the envy of the great and
the admiration of the skilful; a place to be visited by
travellers." It was also a local wonder. No doubt neighbours were puzzled;

> beholding mottos,
> And urns, and domes, and cells, and grottos,
> Folks, little dreaming of the muses,
> Were plagu'd to guess their proper uses;

but they could at least steal the flowers.

Of course Shenstone himself was an attraction, having
achieved a considerable reputation as a poet. The line of
his ballad,

> Oh DAWSON, monarch of my heart,

was as famous as the line, later altered, of Thomson's
tragedy,

> O, Sophonisba, Sophonisba, O!

Of the *School-Mistress* Crabbe could say,

> the Mistress of a village-school
> Became a queen, enthroned upon a stool.

The *Pastoral Ballad* may have been even more popular; it

had the advantage of having been inspired by two ladies, first by Miss G——, then, when the fickle lover met her at Cheltenham, by Miss C——. The trickling rills of The Leasowes may also have inspired the tripping verse:

> Ye shepherds so cheerful and gay,
>   Whose flocks never carelessly roam:
> Should CORYDON'S happen to stray,
>   Oh! call the poor wanderers home.

And the poem was not without charm:

> So sweetly she bade me adieu,
>   I thought that she bade me return.

Then there were the well-known lines, supposed to have been written at Henley-on-Thames because Dr Johnson repeated them at Henley-in-Arden, though in fact they were written at Edge Hill:

> Whoe'er has travell'd life's dull round,
>   Where'er his stages may have been,
> May sigh to think he still has found
>   The warmest welcome, at an inn.

The Doctor, in repeating them "with great emotion," was hardly complimentary to his hospitable friends. Nor was Shenstone to his friend, Anthony Whistler, when he deserted his house for the inn at Edge Hill; but he had lost money at cards, a game he detested, and he had the decency to put the poem in his *Levities*. So with one thing and another Shenstone had won a reputation as a poet; but it was more as a farmer he was esteemed by his distinguished visitors.

As a poet he was not very observant of Nature; it is almost with surprise we come on the lines,

The tangled vetch's purple bloom,
The fragrance of the bean's perfume.

He claimed that in drawing a landskip he fairly drew his picture from the spot, but it was a strange spot of which he could say,

Not a pine in my grove is there seen,
But with tendrils of woodbine is bound.

But as a gardener he shared the new enthusiasm for Nature. The formal garden had long been the fashion; Nature, crushed out of it, was to be brought back, not, however, with its coarse country manners, but with the effect of a well-bred rusticity. With The Leasowes in mind Richard Jago laid down the two principles of the new gardening:

Let no strait terrac'd Lines your Slopes deform;
No barb'rous Walls restrain the bounded Sight.[1]

Nature abhors a straight line. By its abolition Lancelot Brown wrought such an improvement in grounds and gardens that a friend said to him, "I hope I may die before you, so that I may see heaven before you improve it." If a rill was so unnatural as to take a straight course, Shenstone corrected it; as a visitor to his farm said, "the proprieter has taken the Naiad by the hand, and led her an irregular dance into the valley." But the best way of bringing the country into the garden was to do the opposite, bring the garden into the country. When an obstructing wall or fence was replaced by a dry ditch, the ha-ha, the result was wonderful; of Kent, who made great use of the ha-ha, Horace Walpole said, "he leaped the fence, and saw that all nature was a garden." The Leasowes, being

[1] *Edge-hill.*

hilly, had little need of ha-has, but Shenstone, by cutting out of his woods selected viewpoints, included in his farm Halesowen's church steeple, the Clent Hills and distant Welsh mountains. Perhaps Kent went too far in planting dead trees in Kensington Gardens; at least the Londoners thought so, who insisted they should be removed; but in any case Shenstone, who no doubt had dead trees in his wooded dingles, would not be tempted by the example. So by carrying the style of the new garden, *Jardin Anglais*, into his new farm, *Ferme Ornée*, Shenstone made The Leasowes one of the most sensational things in England.

From Graves we gather how the work began. "He had already cut a straight walk through his wood, terminated by a small building of rough stone." The building was an advantage if, as Shenstone thought, "a rural scene is never perfect without the addition of some kind of building." But the *straight* walk! No doubt it was the walk to which Dodsley refers: "though the walk, as I said, is strait-lined, yet the base rises and falls so agreeably as leaves no room to censure it's formality." And Shenstone may have improved it with the addition of ruts and stones, a common practice. Then Graves goes on: "And in a sort of gravel or marle-pit, in the corner of a field, amongst some hazels, he had scooped out a sort of cave, stuck a little cross of wood over the door, and called it an hermitage." Here again he would not follow the example of Kent, who for his Hermit's Cave at Pain's Hill in Surrey hired a hermit, at least a poor creature clad like one and with the accessories. After the hermitage began what Graves calls "Mr Shenstone's commerce with the water-nymphs." This might seem to amount to little more than the diverting of a rill to make small waterfalls as it ran down a wooded dingle. But there was much more; Shenstone could see,

> Where the green Dryads guard his woods,
> Where the blue Naiads guide his floods.

For they were very real to him; their disarrangement in winter distressed him; "to see the nakedness of our beloved mistresses, the Naiads and the Dryads, exposed by that ruffian Winter to universal observation, is a severity scarcely to be supported by the help of blazing hearths, cheerful companions, and a bottle of the most grateful burgundy." So he kept on improving his farm, adding here an urn in memory of a friend, and there a pyramid, an even more solemn ornament. "The French have what they call a *parque-ornée*; I gave my place the title of a *ferme-ornée*."

Some of Shenstone's ideas seem odd; he admits a house into a landskip; indeed, it brings its own welcome; but he will not admit a hedge. "Hedges appearing as such, are universally bad; they discover art in nature's province." Yet in *Essays on Men, Manners, and Things* he shows a witty common sense; he proves in himself the truth of one of his sayings, "A person is something taller by holding up his head," but not the truth of another, "A fool and his words are easily parted." He writes in a plain style, not practising what he condemns in others, "the trade, the *craft*—to write obscurely." And there are his *Letters*, the best to Lady Luxborough, with whom he exchanged so much correspondence that she suggested the starting of a service of carrier-pigeons. She was a lady of refinement, who could understand him when he said, "Melancholy has and ever had its charms for Persons of ye finest Taste." No doubt it had, for in Henry Mackenzie's *The Man of Feeling* have been counted fifty instances of an outburst of tears. At the same time she could appreciate his practical advice, "Why don't your Ladyship throw all yr Haystacks into ye Form of Pyramids, and chuse out places where they may look agreeably?" Burns speaks of Shenstone as "that celebrated Poet, whose divine Elegies do honour to our nation, our language, and our species";[1] he was even better as a letter-writer.

But best of all, in his own view at least, was Shenstone as a farmer; he had created the *Ferme Ornée*. So artfully was it designed that he insisted on conducting visitors over it himself, annoyed when his neighbour, Lord Lyttelton, suffering from gout, took short cuts. No doubt he was right, if visitors were to observe with Graves "with what happy dexterity Mr Shenstone conducted the Naiads through his groves." There were many seats, which could of course be occupied, though they were, as Dodsley explains, mainly intended as hints to spectators not to let something escape their notice. Perhaps he lent his visitors Claude-glasses, small convex mirrors, tinted with two or three colours, which tinged the reflected scene with soft hues; they were much used by travellers, by Gray, for example, when he visited the Lake Country. "I am going to procure a Convex Glass to see the Landskip with," Shenstone wrote to Lady Luxborough. Various objects were met on the way, a Temple of Pan, a ruinated Priory occupied by a farm-worker, root-houses, not for storing turnips but for orna-ment, being mostly made of tree-roots, romantic cascades, one so remarkable that Dodsley could say, "it is not but upon reflection that we find the stream is not a Niagara, but rather a waterfal in miniature." But above all was Virgil's Grove; "many parts of my Farm were extrava-gantly commended, but the Grove especially," Shenstone wrote to Lady Luxborough. A place of gloom, where little

[1] Preface to the Kilmarnock Edition.

was visible, it best carried out his idea, "Art should never be allowed to set a foot in the province of nature, otherwise than clandestinely and by night." But that was true of The Leasowes as a whole; there was no appearance of the artificial about the farm; Lady Luxborough could commend it as a case of the art that Nature conceals,

> Where she triumphant claims the total plan,
> And, with fresh pride, adopts the work of man.

Shenstone congratulated himself on being a planter, not a builder; what was built began at once to decay, what was planted to improve. But it is a disconsolate ghost who now wanders over a golf-course. Though the dingles remain, he listens to no voices saying,

> Here in cool grot, and mossy cell,
> We rural fays and faeries dwell.

But the melancholy he feels as a ghost is not different in kind from the melancholy he cultivated on his farm. We may say of him and the distinguished visitors who approved of his farm methods, that with almost everything in life to gratify them they took their pleasures sadly. Shenstone would have replied that there was no other way of taking what was transitory. "The words 'no more' have a singular pathos."

Selborne

MOSES HARRIS, a contemporary of Gilbert White, accounting for a butterfly's name, Glanvil Fritillaria, tells a story in *The Aurelian*. "This Fly took its name from the ingenious Lady Glanvil, whose Memory had like to have suffered from her Curiosity. Some Relations that were disappointed by her Will, attempted to set it aside by Acts of Lunacy, for they suggested that none but those who were deprived of their Senses, would go in pursuit of Butterflies. Her Relations and Legatees subpoened Dr Sloane and Mr Ray to support her Character. The last Gentleman went to Exeter, and in the Tryal satisfied the Judge and Jury of the Lady's laudable Inquiry into the wonderful Works of the Creation, and established her Will." That an interest in natural history, regarded in Lady Glanvil's time as almost a form of madness, has become so popular is in large part due to Gilbert White's *Natural History of Selborne.*

Here was a book on natural history that people could read. A certain Mr Davies, a Cambridge don, to whom Crabbe showed his manuscript of a botanical treatise, was so shocked that it should be written in English, not in Latin, an insult to the science, that the poet, feeling the rebuff, laid it aside and, never finished, it was burnt with other papers.[1] Gilbert White had some excuse for his *Natural History* being in English; it is composed of letters

[1] *Life, by his Son.*

written to friends and afterwards published. For another thing he showed people an attractive way of pursuing the science. Going out into the open, often no further than his own garden, he made what he called autopsias. Sometimes they were post-mortems; "many times have I had the curiosity to open the stomachs of woodcocks and snipes"; but usually an autopsia was no more than what the word literally means, a personal observation. Of course it had to be correct; it would not have been a true autopsia to see that his neighbour's peacocks had brightly coloured tails, for peacocks have no such tails, though he must often have heard they had; but it was a true autopsia to notice that their gorgeous trains grew from their backs, the actual tails consisting of stiff quills. He taught people to look with their eyes, not with their ears. But he also taught them not to be content with a bare observation of facts, but inquisitively to seek their explanation. The peacocks' trains, for example, he explained as a device to attract the peahens. "These birds can make the shafts of their long feathers clatter like the swords of a sword-dancer; they then trample very quick with their feet, and run backwards towards the females." "What make ye of Parson White in Selborne?" asks Thomas Carlyle.[1] But the answer was already given; for once people were seeing in the Parson a good example and following it themselves.

A remarkable thing about Gilbert White's *Natural History* is that it has not gone out of date. Most books of the kind share the fate of "the awful repository of all the errors of antiquity," as Isaac Disraeli called Pliny's *Natural History*. Dr Johnson, hearing that Goldsmith was writing a natural history, said, "he will make it as entertaining as a Persian tale"; but all the creatures in that *Animated*

[1] *Essay on Biography.*

G

Nature are long since dead, while Timothy, Gilbert White's tortoise, is still alive in spite of its "arbitrary stomach," even in spite of the fact that its shell is in South Kensington Museum. An Oxford don, so far from objecting to the book being written in English, made the prophecy to a nephew of Gilbert White, "depend upon it, the time will come when very few who buy books will be without it," a rare case of a literary prophecy coming true. Another remarkable thing is that the book is read, and even loved, by people who have little or no interest in natural history. They find in it, of course, a few things curious and memorable. The parlour cat, becoming electric in Siberian weather, may give them a pleasant little shock. They smile indulgently at the description of the South Downs, "that chain of majestic mountains," forgetting that in Gilbert White's time a mountain might be of no great size; Bunyan speaks of a man "who stumbled and fell in a wide field, full of dark mountains." But pleasantries apart, what, in general, is the book about? The bestial creation, as the writer calls it, particularly "the life and conversation" of birds, with a few parochial matters. The Gallios, who care for none of these things, might think the *Journal* in which he first wrote down his observations was, in more senses than one, a commonplace book.

Perhaps it is to Gilbert White as writer, rather than as naturalist, that this natural history owes its popular success. "Owls move in a buoyant manner, as if lighter than the air . . . crows and daws swagger in their walk . . . herons seem encumbered with too much sail for their light bodies, but these vast hollow wings are necessary in carrying burdens, such as large fishes . . . the king-fisher darts along like an arrow"; Coleridge comments on this descriptive passage, "The matter disappointed me; I have myself made and collected a better table of characters of flight and motion." But that is hard to believe; these simple words have a visual quality; in reading them, it is the birds we see, not the pages of a book. But if that passage did not please Coleridge, he might have delighted in the passage about the house-crickets, "particularly fond of kitchens and bakers' ovens, on account of their perpetual warmth. Tender insects that live abroad either enjoy only the short period of one summer, or else doze away the cold uncomfortable months in profound slumbers; but these, residing as it were in a torrid zone, are always alert and merry,—a good Christmas fire is to them like the heats of the dog-days." Gilbert White thought the *Georgics* "the most beautiful of all human compositions," and Virgil's bees may have been buzzing in his memory when he wrote in that fanciful way of the crickets. It was not his usual style; in his walks about Selborne he seldom came, following another parson, George Herbert,

> to phansies medow strow'd
> With many a flower.

His botanical studies did not include flowers of speech. Though he wrote verses, this clear-sighted naturalist was not one of those poets of whom David Hume makes fun, saying they are like the angels who cover their eyes with their wings.

But the great virtue of Gilbert White's writing is that it is so communicative of himself. No doubt he was modest; "my little intelligence is confined to the narrow sphere of my observations at home"; yet in writing about birds, beetles and grasshoppers, he is all the time writing about himself. The book is an autobiography, all the better for not being one. What Boswell said of Addison could be said with more meaning of Gilbert White, "he wrote with the ease of a gentleman; his readers feel that a wise and accomplished companion is talking to them." And his company and talk are the more intimate because it is on a small stage the intercourse takes place, Selborne, "a poor pelting village," and its purlieus. We almost grudge his leaving it to visit relations in Sussex, though its chain of majestic mountains he investigated with fresh admiration year by year. Yet of these relations and others, and also of his friends, he has so little to say that we feel we almost have him to ourselves. Of course the half of Gilbert White is not told in the book. We have to gather elsewhere that he was social, entertaining much at home and paying frequent visits, so very social in his Oriel days that he was nicknamed the Busser. And he was not so intellectually isolated as we might imagine. He had two friends, famous botanists, living within a few miles; at Alton was Curtis, who caught his love of plants from John Lagg, ostler at the Crown Inn, and at Faringdon Stephen Hales, among whose many useful and benevolent works was, says Gilbert White in a letter, "his teaching the house-wife to place an inverted tea-cup at the bottom of her pies and tarts." Yet the Gilbert White of the book is so closely associated with Selborne that in visiting the village we almost feel that we are paying a personal call on the vicar, forgetting for the moment he was only curate.

Russell Lowell, after visiting Selborne and its purlieus, paid a good compliment to the writer of *Natural History*: "I still see them through his eyes rather than by any recollection of actual and personal vision."[1] It seems to make a visit to Selborne superfluous. But we should not offhand refuse *The Invitation*:

[1] *My Garden Acquaintances.*

See, Selborne spreads her boldest beauties round,
The varied valley, and the mountain ground,
Wildly majestic!

We are not likely to be disappointed with the mountain,
though it is only a small hill, miscalled the Hanger, a name
properly belonging to the hanging beech-wood. We shall
feel Gilbert White has imparted something of himself to
the scene,

A noble spirit in a hill,
A human touch about a tree.[1]

And certainly the hill is striking; with its individuality
you may not realise it is only an escarpment of the Hampshire Downs until you slip on its chalk on a damp day.
That is likely to be on the Zigzag, a track that from a
distance darts up the slope like forked lightning. Gilbert
helped his brother to make it, at least with money, and also
brought from Faringdon, where for a long time he was
curate, the sarsen at the summit, but not the name with its
superstition, Wishing Stone. But before reaching the summit, you will have paused to gaze down on Selborne itself,
a prospect that might remind you of what Cobbett said to
the farmer, "People ought to be happy here, for that God
has done everything for them."

But while the setting remains the same, Cobbett could
not now say, "The village of Selborne is precisely what it
is described by Mr. White." Even the two important
buildings are much altered, his grandfather's vicarage
where he was born, and the house, the Wakes, where he
lived and wrote. The latter is now his memorial; it looks
too tidy; articles are not laid out with a careful casualness,
waiting the revenant, as in the home of another naturalist,

[1] Coventry Patmore.

Darwin's at Downe. With so little to suggest Gilbert
White, you may fall back on your memory of some incident
that happened in the house. There was, for example, the
occasion when he asked a servant how he had broken a
glass; his thirst for explanation must have been more than
satisfied when the old man, fetching another glass, showed
him how by letting it fall on the floor.

The Plestor keeps better its old character. Originally the
market-place of the Priory monks, it now answers to its
name, which means Play-place. The stag-headed sycamore
supplanted a famous oak that Gilbert White wrote about
but never saw, for it fell before his time, a victim to the
Great Storm of November 1703. Macaulay tells of the
astounding effects of the storm: "Large mansions had been
blown down. One Prelate had been buried beneath the
ruins of his palace. London and Bristol had presented the
appearance of cities just sacked."[1] But yews are said never
to fall, and the oak's contemporary, the churchyard yew,
survived the storm. In a county noted for its yews it is a
good example of a "Hampshire weed." Though its long
arms need support, so that it looks like an octopus leaning
on sticks, it is far from decrepit, not one of those trees,

> Whose wooden Carcasses are grown
> To be but coffins.[2]

It puts to shame the four lime trees Gilbert White planted
to screen a butcher's yard, one now entirely gone and the
others hollow and black like chimneys. He calculated that
it might have seen several centuries, a cautious estimate,
showing a lack of the usual credulity about the age of yews.
It set his inquiring mind speculating as to the uses served
by churchyard yews; he thought they may have provided

---

[1] *Essay on Addison.*   [2] Cleveland.

bows for archery and screened the church from violent winds, two uses they were occasionally intended to serve. Of course he could not fail to see in the dark foliage an emblem of mortality; so it had been since Juno descended into Hades by a path shaded with deadly yews;[1] but it is strange a parson did not see that the foliage, being evergreen, made it equally well an emblem of immortality.

The church is of no special interest apart from Gilbert White who, strangely enough, was curate there three times, though on the first two occasions for less than a year. The interior has an odd look, the Norman pillars somewhat squat and their capitals like crushed cushions. But odder in a way is the Gilbert White Memorial Window, its subject St Francis preaching to the birds. It was not to birds this curate preached; they would no more have listened to him than his congregation, had he entered the pulpit threatening them with a gun. We gather that latterly he gave up the gun, calling the birds "little sisters." He may also have given up asking his friends to procure him specimens, realising that his acquaintance with his little sisters did not become more intimate by examining the contents of their stomachs. He had come to share the new and more sentimental approach to Nature of his time. For the sentiment was not confined to poets; the philosopher Kant, having held a swallow in his hand and looked into its eyes, said, "As I gazed, it was as if I had seen into heaven." Sentimental is not nowadays a popular word except in a poor sense, yet any approach to Nature that is without feeling is a going farther away;

> The ones that cite her most
> Have never passed her haunted house,
> Nor simplified her ghost.[2]

[1] Ovid, *Metamorphoses*.   [2] Emily Dickinson.

There can be no purely factual interest in birds, for the subject of the interest would not be—*birds*. Nor can there be a collection of *butterflies*. We do not know much about Lady Glanvil, but if she collected butterflies, thinking they were *butterflies* she collected, the verdict of the jury, that she was in her right mind, is open to question.

Yardley Oak

ABOUT all I remembered of Olney was how to pro-
nounce the name: it rhymes with pony. There were
circus ponies in the water-meadow as I crossed the bridge,
but I was not poetically inspired. That Olney was so
pleasant a place I had no idea. If it is not uncomplimentary
to a town to say it looks old-fashioned, I should say it of
Olney; I could imagine women still making the lace for
which it was famous, the "needlework sublime." In the
long grey street and market-place there was hardly an
ugly building except Cowper's house; that, I felt, deserved
to be turned into a museum. Yet it was dear to poor
Cowper; as he wrote to Newton, "it is the place of all the
world I love the most, not for any happiness it affords me,
but because here I can be miserable with most convenience
to myself and with least disturbance to others."

Nor did I know Olney had so charming a pendant in a
small village about a mile away, Weston Underwood.
Mrs Unwin and Mr Cowper, as she always called him,
used to walk to it each day, when the weather permitted.
They took a road that rises to overlook the wide green
valley of the Ouse, a river

That, as with molten glass, inlays the vale.

It might have been called Ouse because it winds its round-
about way so slowly; even when it was hurrying under
Olney bridge, I thought of the woman in Middleton's play
who was told,

> nothing comes nimbly from you;
> You dance like a plumber's daughter.

To the pedestrian on the high road it discloses itself in erratic silver streaks;

> The Ouse, dividing the well-water'd land,
> Now glitters in the sun, and now retires,
> As bashful, yet impatient to be seen.

Cowper is even more fanciful about a rill farther on the switchback road:

> Hence the declivity is sharp and short,
> And such the reascent; between them weeps
> A little naiad her impoverish'd urn
> All summer long, which winter fills again.

It is a sluttish naiad who tilts her urn there now. These daily walks, weather permitting, came to an end when they went to live in Weston Underwood. "It is one of the prettiest villages in England," Cowper used to write to his friends. He could not have known many English villages, for he says, "I have not been more than thirteen miles from home these twenty years"; but the statement can stand. If I was surprised at having to enter a village by an imposing stone gateway, yet, having entered and looked around, I thought it a well-deserved prelude. Cowper's house is near Cowper's Oak, an inn to which I was directed several times the following day, when all I wanted to find was a tree.

The memory of a magic night in Yardley Chase, when I walked by moonlit rides, had brought me back to Olney, though I also alleged as a reason that I ought to see Yardley Oak. It was not a good reason, for I knew I could not see it; it was dead, even cremated. Some children a few years before had made a fire in its hollow trunk;

A huge throat, calling to the clouds for drink,

it had called that day in vain and the tree was burnt to the ground. But I could at least shed a tear over its ashes, if, as Blake says, a tear is an intellectual thing.

Local maps and people call it Cowper's Oak. Perhaps it got the name even in the poet's lifetime, being, as he says, "an oak which I often visit, and which is one of the wonders that I show to all who come this way." He goes on, "I tell them all that it is a thousand years old, verily believing it to be so, though I do not know it." Very likely it was; Dryden's biographical sketch of an old oak,

> Three centuries he grows, and three he stays,
> Supreme in state, and in three more decays,

is thought to be more or less true. The oak is one of the few trees, the yew and chestnut being others, which may justify Evelyn's name, Methuselahs. But more probably the name, Cowper's Oak, is due to its being the subject of the poem, *Yardley Oak*.

What the poet thinks of the tree, we might think of the poem: it was fortunate to see the light of day. A thievish jay might have eaten the whole tree as an acorn,

> swallowing down
> Thy yet close-folded latitude of boughs
> And all thine embryo vastness at a gulp;

the poem, left by the despondent poet in a wastepaper-basket, might have escaped Hayley's eye. His friend was so astonished by the recovery of this great, but abandoned, poem that he said, "I could hardly have been more surprised if a noble oak, in its natural majesty, had started up from the turf of my garden with full foliage before me." Yet it is only a fragment of a poem which Cowper may have felt unable to finish. Already there is a falling away in the passage where he left off; it is about Adam, and amounts to even less than the statement in the *Golden Legend*, "he was thirty years of age, when he was but a day old." He misses the usual description of Adam, "the man without a navel"; or perhaps he did not think it poetical.

Yardley Chase, which I entered near Denton, intending to take the tree on my way back to Olney, was disappointing. The memory of the moonlit walk by rides, was it mostly moonshine? There were plenty of rides; I even invented a name for walking along them, I called it riding. But they were straight, narrow and ditched, and all they awoke in me was a lovesick recollection of the New Forest. Only snowy conditions could have lent enchantment to the view, and I thought of Cowper's description of the snow-bound landscape, where the patient reader feels that the long poem for a few pages belies its name, *The Task*. And though it was winter, I might have heard the nightingale! For has he not a poem, *To the Nightingale, Which the Author heard sing on New Year's Day*? There were no remarkable trees such as one expects in an ancient chase, or, if there were, it was a case of not seeing the trees for the wood. Nothing suggested animals being chased except the withered bodies of stoats, skin and skeleton, that hung from trees, dancing in the wind like long-legged ballerinas. Yet the chase improved for a time when it opened out in a noble glade, where scattered oaks had room to stretch their arms. The boughs naked, the trunks looked like rivers standing on end, their tributaries in the air. I disturbed a herd of fallow deer, two of them not fallow but white. Perhaps one of their ancestors made the cradle for that baby, the acorn, that grew to be Yardley Oak, if, as Cowper suggests,

> a skipping deer
> With pointed hoof dibbling the glebe, prepared
> The soft receptacle.

Naturally I thought of that other passage in *The Task*:

> I was a stricken deer, that left the herd
> Long since. With many an arrow deep infix'd
> My panting side was charged, when I withdrew
> To seek a tranquil death in distant shades.
> There was I found by one, who had himself
> Been hurt by th'archers.

Here I began to ask my way to Cowper's Oak, the tree, not the inn, mostly of woodmen going home from their work. Directions differed widely, but there was a consensus of opinion that I should strike a concrete road, which would take me to the spot. That seemed odd; was Cowper so popular a poet that it needed such a road to carry the traffic to this shrine? I was glad after a time to think I was more or less in the right way; I had caught sight of those giants, Gog and Magog.

Yet at first I was startled by their forbidding appearance, as Dante was by the giants he took for towers in the ninth circle of the *Inferno*. They had a somewhat sinister look, as though like Virgil's oak their roots reached as far down to Tartarus as their foliage rose to the airs of heaven. It was even queer that in spite of their great age they stood so erect, rising above their younger neighbours; if Ossian's hero, the King of Inis-thona, had seen such trees, he would hardly have made the strange statement, "I bend like the trunk of an aged oak." Gog had changed his sex, for in Cowper's time he, or rather she, was called Judith, no doubt after William the Conqueror's niece, who owned part of the chase. Gog seemed the more suitable name for the monster, yet less because he was larger than the lady than because he looked much stupider. But, after all, Dodona's oak was the only tree intelligent enough to talk, and I respected Gog for his great age. I applied to him the words borrowed from *Yardley Oak*:

Time was, when, settling on thy leaf, a fly
Could shake thee to the root—and time has been
When tempests could not.

But where was Cowper's Oak? Somehow I had imagined that because he speaks of the two trees in the same letter, they must be near each other; but that was foolish, they might be miles apart. And I remembered another letter in which he tells how on two occasions he set out for Judith, but went no farther than his own tree, his reason the first time being that the weather was too warm and the second time too wet. I was thinking these were strange reasons for one who claimed to have excelled at both cricket and football, when I struck the concrete road. I could not have avoided it, as it stretched across the chase, evidently made by soldiers. It ended in one direction in a road marked Private, in the other in a road which did not need to be marked Public. It was the latter I took, back to Olney.

It was not till next day I could say I had seen the tree, quite early in the morning. As I slept in Cowper's room at The Bull, I felt it was the poet himself who showed it; indeed, it was, as he had often shown it before. For it resembled the Phoenix in rising to a new life. Yet the two were different; the Arabian bird, having martyred herself, sprang from her ashes to live for another five hundred years; the tree, anticipating its fiery death at the hands of children, achieved what appears to be an unconditioned immortality. I was seeing it plain as print, when a young man, bringing in my morning tea, said, "You are reading already."

The Loves of the Plants

WHEN Augusta said to her Preceptor Husband, in Crabbe's tale,

> "Stigma! I know,—the things with yellow heads,
> That shed the dust, and grow upon the threads,"

it was no wonder he dolefully closed the botany book. She did not know the difference between a stigma and a stamen! Yet he had tried to explain in a pleasant way, as she admitted:

> "You call them wives and husbands, but you know
> That is a joke."

She had found botany dull as she had also found history. When she saw he was wondering how she spent her time,

> "Oh! you believe," said she, "that other things
> Are read as well as histories of kings,
> And loves of plants, with all that simple stuff
> About their sex, of which I know enough."

She admitted she had been reading *Wanderings of the Heart* and *Haunted Hall*. She hastened to explain that she also read Pope and Milton, but to her "Are you satisfied?" he coldly replied, "Entirely, madam!"[1]

One has a good deal of sympathy with Augusta Finch. When a woman is taken for a walk by her husband, she may not care to have the different leaf-formations shown to her,

[1] *Tales of the Hall.*

> Panduriform, pinnatifid, premorse,
> Latent, and patent, papulous, and plane;

it was no wonder,

> "Oh!" said the pupil, "it will turn my brain."

What Finch should have done was to buy her a copy of Erasmus Darwin's *Botanic Garden*. She read Pope; Darwin wrote verse that ran more smoothly than Pope's; it almost ran off the page. She read Milton; the *Botanic Garden* was an epic that in some ways resembled *Paradise Lost*; at least it contained an account of Creation and the description of a garden. And its purpose was to give instruction in botany in an attractive way; as Darwin explains, "the general design is to inlist Imagination under the banner of Science, to induce the ingenious to cultivate the knowledge of Botany." She had no need to be afraid of "the banner of Science"; it was a flag waving, "GENTLE READER! walk in, and view the wonders of my INCHANTED GARDEN." She would find herself in good company: "The Muses are young Ladies; we expect to see them dressed; though not like some modern beauties, with so much gauze and feather, that the Lady herself is the least part of her." If Finch had any feeling for poetry, he could have recommended the *Botanic Garden* to Augusta as Horace Walpole did to the Misses Berry, "in short, all, all, all, is the most lovely Poetry."[1]

The *Botanic Garden* is in two parts; the second, *The Loves of the Plants*, is the one that would most concern Augusta. For here Darwin's method is simple; he does, or rather undoes, what Ovid did in the *Metamorphoses*. "Whereas Ovid did by art poetic transmute Men, Women,

[1] *Letters.*

and even Gods and Goddesses, into Trees and Flowers; I
have undertaken by similar art to restore some of them
to their original animality, after having remained prisoners
so long in their respective vegetable mansions." That
would have been a relief to the Heliades, Phaethon's sisters
once, but changed to poplars, "for ever weeping for a
brother's death." But they are not changed back, nor are
oak and linden changed back to Philemon and Baucis.
Darwin hardly keeps his promise, almost all his changes
being in plants that need no change. Yet sometimes the
change is a happy one, as in the case of the snowdrop:

> bright GALANTHA glows,
> And prints with frolic step the melting snows.

The intention is to bring out the plant's character. Wordsworth has a different idea of it when he speaks of snowdrops
nodding their helmets and compares them for hardihood
with the Emathian phalanx, but Darwin was the better
botanist. Certainly no exception can be taken to the change
in the case of impatiens or touch-me-not. It is a plant,
Coles says, "near which if you put your hand, the Seed will
spurtle forth suddenly, in so much that the unexpectednesse
of it made the valiant Lord *Fairfax* to start."[1] The
metamorphosed plant loses nothing of its character:

> With fierce distracted eye IMPATIENS stands,
> Swells her pale cheeks, and brandishes her hands,
> With rage and hate the astonish'd groves alarms,
> And hurls her infants from her frantic arms.

The vine, one of Ovid's plants, acquires a heightened, or
rather lowered, character in being restored to its animality,
as, indeed, we might expect.

[1] *The Art of Simpling.*

H

Drunk with her own rich Juice, she cannot stand,

Cowley says of the vineyard plant;[1] in the *Botanic Garden*
she becomes a tempter:

"Drink deep, sweet youths," seductive VITIS cries,
The maudlin tear-drop glittering in her eyes.

Part of Darwin's botany would be already familiar to
Augusta, for like Finch he changes stamens and stigmas
into men and women, though not in a joke.

Sweet blooms GENISTA in the myrtle shade,
And *ten* fond brothers woo the haughty maid.

No doubt she is haughty because she does not wish to be
wooed by one of her own household; she believes in cross-
pollination. But much would be new and attractive to
Augusta. If her taste was for sentimental tales like
Wanderings of the Heart, she could not fail to be touched by
the case of the cyclamen. "When the seeds are ripe, the
stalk of the flower gradually twists itself spirally down-
wards, till it touches the ground, and penetrating the earth,
lodges its seeds." So Darwin says in an explanatory note
to the poem; but in the poem itself the plant is a mother
bereaved of her child:

The gentle CYCLAMEN with dewy eye
Breathes o'er her lifeless babe the parting sigh;
And, bending low to earth, with pious hands
Inhumes her dear Departed in the sands.

If Augusta's taste was for frightening tales like *Haunted
Hall*, she would have enjoyed the passage about Medea.
RUBIA, who is metamorphosed madder, a plant used in
dyeing, is compared with the Witch. As RUBIA bends

[1] *Liber Plantarum.*

over a cauldron in which she stains white fleeces, so Medea bent over a cauldron in which floated her old father-in-law, restoring him to youth by her magic herbs. Of this passage Horace Walpole said, "It seized hold of my imagination, that my blood thrilled back through my veins, and my hair broke the cementing of the friseur to gain the attitude of horror."

Yet, after all, Augusta might not have appreciated the *Botanic Garden*; if her literary taste was at all conventional, it would appear disconcertingly modern. It had broken with tradition, the abstractions of eighteenth-century verse replaced by sensational images. Young Wordsworth extolled it, though later, so many of its comparisons beginning with "So," he called it a so-so poem. Coleridge regarded Darwin as "the first literary character in Europe," meaning the one who had made the greatest stir. Yet Charles Darwin says, "no one of the present generation reads, as it appears, a single line of it." Perhaps he was wrong; he might in any case have spoken in a pleasanter way about his grandfather's poem. Erasmus Darwin was in many ways a remarkable man, with a greater range of knowledge than any man in Europe, Coleridge thought; and he undertook an astounding task, to turn the Linnaean system of botany into poetry. If like so many poems extolled as modern in their day it proved a failure, it was at least a GREAT failure.

The Reverend
George Crabbe

THE name Aldborough, Old Fortress, has changed to
Aldeburgh, Town on the Alde, as though to suit the
place's smarter appearance. For an East Coast town it is
strangely attractive; its buildings have variety and colour,
and the street facing the sea has a cheerful, even jaunty air.
The town remembers the sea's savage attacks, but the
innumerable missiles slung at it have become its own
defence, a raised stone beach. With the further fortification
of a low grim wall there can be no such disaster as Crabbe's
father remembered, eleven houses demolished by a spring
tide: "he saw the breakers dash over the roofs, curl around
the walls, and crush all to ruin." That was in the old town,
which has suffered a sea-change, the market-place under
water, fishes swimming where fishes were sold, and the
Moot Hall, once at the centre of things, now so close to
the beach that it might be the mayor's bathing-house.
Inside it is a map, showing the old town; we see it better
in Crabbe's poems, *The Village* and *The Borough*.

Aldborough was a town of some importance; probably
Crabbe's reason for reducing it to a village was to contrast
his poem with Goldsmith's *Deserted Village*; that poem
gave a conventional, even sentimental picture of village
life, here was the real thing. He was also contrasting it
with those poems in which shepherds

their amorous pains reveal,
The only pains, alas! they never feel,

poems such as the *Pastorals* of Ambrose Philips, out of
whose name the word "namby-pamby" was coined. *The
Village*, being realistic, was something new, and, as the
wise Telemachus said to his mother, Penelope, "men
praise that song the most which comes newest to their
ears." It was so successful a novelty that Shackleton,
Burke's friend, said that Goldsmith's poem, once so
popular, would now be the deserted *Village*.

The poem hardly suggests what Shackleton called
Crabbe himself, "the youth with the *sour* name and the
sweet countenance." His face does not light up as he views
the village. But the scene is not Arcadian:

No; cast by Fortune on a frowning coast,
Which neither groves nor happy valleys boast;
Where other cares than those the Muse relates

(not, however, a care for grammar)

And other shepherds dwell with other mates;
By such examples taught, I paint the Cot.

And he paints it, as Hazlitt said, "like a man sent to dis-
train for rent." And the villagers! How could he view them
with a sweet countenance?

Here joyless roam a wild amphibious race,
With sullen woe display'd in every face.

And how depressing is the heath behind,

Where the thin harvest waves its wither'd ears.

No doubt there are flowers, such as charlock, blue bugloss
and slimy mallow, but their effect is not cheerful; they
mingle their tints,

And a sad splendour vainly shines around.
So looks the nymph whom wretched arts adorn,
Betray'd by man, then left for man to scorn.

Crabbe might have said of *The Village* what he said of the
later *Parish Register*,

> When from the cradle to the grave I look,
> Mine I conceive a melancholy book.

The Village was followed by *The Borough*. There was a
long interval between them, more than twenty years, as
though explaining how a village came to grow into a
borough. The town now includes Slaughden Quay, less
than a mile away, a place still little changed since young
Crabbe worked there as a day labourer. Here the Alde
behaves in a remarkable way; in sight of the sea, if it could
peer over the intervening bank, it suddenly changes its
mind, and turns to flow for ten miles along the coast,
where, changing its name, it becomes the Ore. On one side
is a long stretch of stony beach where Crabbe found the
washed-up dogs he dissected when studying to be a doctor;
on the other side are the poor meadows with brackish
ditches where he found the herbs he used in his practice.
The dogs may have taught him anatomy, but his fear of
operating made him fail as a doctor and give up his practice.
But the practice in any case was not remunerative, for, as
his son explains, "his ignorant patients, seeing him
return from his walks with handfuls of weeds, decided that,
as Dr Crabbe got his medicines in the ditches, he could
have little claim for payment."

The Borough is a better poem than *The Village*, but it
shows no improvement in the townsfolk. Certainly when
Crabbe, having been ordained, came among them as curate
of the parish church, they did not view him with a sweet

countenance. That was evident from his first sermon: "I saw unfriendly faces about me." Yet at the end of *The Borough* he disclaims any prejudice against them:

> Nor be it ever of my portraits told,—
> "Here the strong lines of malice we behold."

Nor has the place improved more than the people; we have to pick our way along polluted paths among ashy heaps and plashy pools. It suffers from a sad monotony; the only thing that brings a little life to it is the burial of a pauper:

> The day itself is, like the night, asleep;
> Or, on the sameness if a break be made,
> 'Tis by some pauper to his grave convey'd.

No doubt it is pleasant to watch the children playing their patriotic games:

> Rodneys in rags here British valour boast,
> And lisping Nelsons fright the Gallic coast;
> They fix the rudder, set the swelling sail,
> They point the bowsprit, and they blow the gale.

Yet the poor creatures are in danger of losing their lives, not in a naval engagement, but from eating the too attractive berries of henbane and deadly nightshade. One would have thought such poisonous plants would not be left growing where children played. And some of the people must have kept hens. Perhaps the borough and burghers were not as bad as Crabbe painted them.

Crabbe's diary shows he had a natural and sincere piety, yet the philosophy of life expressed in the poems is pessimistic. Even in *Infancy* we see it:

> Alas! and what is earthly good? 'tis lent
> Evil to hide, to soften, to prevent.

One might have imagined that some good existed in its own right;

> No! there is not a joy beneath the skies,
> That from no grief nor trouble shall arise.

We seldom see a smile on Crabbe's countenance; indeed, as in the case of the poor merchant in *Resentment*, a smile

> Would seem incongruous as a singing tree.

Of course there is nothing incongruous about such a tree on a May morning, but no birds sing in Crabbe's poems. Yet Shackleton could not have thought him a pessimist, the youth with the sweet countenance, nor his familiar friends, who found him genial, still less the ladies to whom in his old age he wrote philandering letters. Jane Austen thought she could have married him. Country parson, paterfamilias, lion of London society, as none of these was he the pessimist, but only as poet. His pessimism was a reaction against what he felt was false in other poets, the sentimentality of Ambrose Philips or the optimism of Pope,

> One truth is clear, Whatever is, is right.

The Lover's Journey suggests the foolishness of reading one's own feelings into Nature. Crossing a poor bare heath in the hope of meeting his mistress,

> "How lovely this!" the rapt Orlando said;

later, a dejected lover, riding by a river with flowery banks,

> "I hate these scenes," Orlando angry cried.

Crabbe aimed at being an objective poet; as to Peter Bell,

> A primrose by a river's brim
> A yellow primrose was to him,
> And it was nothing more,

except, of course, a specimen, thrum-eyed or pin-eyed, of *Primula vulgaris*. It is suggestive that his chief botanical interest was in grasses;

> That bridal bed the vulgar term a flower

appealed to him less. He would have approved of the emendation that gives sound sense to a passage of Shakespeare,

> sermons in books,
> Stones in the running brooks.

Parson Crabbe was the preacher, not Nature. One wonders if he allowed his choir to sing the *Benedicite*, "O all ye Works of the Lord, bless ye the Lord: praise him, and magnify him for ever."

Yet Crabbe does not view things objectively when he looks through the eyes of his characters. Villars, indulging his spleen, sees in marsh and heath and sea "one level sadness!" For the lover who rose early

> and look'd with many a sigh
> On the red light that fill'd the eastern sky,

the view was ominous;

> he ponder'd for a while,
> Then met his Fanny with a borrow'd smile.

Nor is he always objective when he looks through his own eyes. A long low stretch of beach fading in hazy distance he calls "a frowning coast"; he is projecting into it the memory of his hard work on Slaughden Quay, or his dislike of the natives,

> Who scowl at strangers with suspicious eye.

And he is almost perverse in what he chooses to view, that

"frowning coast" of Suffolk rather than its smiling inland pastures among which he lived so long. That it was more or less Constable's country brings out the truth of his son's saying, "he had no real love for what a painter's eye considers as the beauties of landscape."

Yet he had a painter's eye—or was it a poet's?—for the beauties of seascape with phosphorescent waves:

> Cast but a stone, or strike them with an oar,
> And you shall flames within the deep explore;
> Or scoop the stream phosphoric as you stand,
> And the cold flames shall flash along your hand;
> When lost in wonder, you shall walk and gaze
> On weeds that sparkle, and on waves that blaze.

So he might have written about the beauties of landscape. But a landscape, for whom was it beautiful? Or a river or a blossoming tree or a flower? Not for his fishermen or smugglers or farm-labourers or inmates of the borough workhouse. Perhaps we should credit Crabbe with a humanitarian feeling for people, even for the scowling burghers, that made him make little use of the painter's eye and take up what may seem so negative an attitude to Nature. When he shows no love for Nature, he shows what is better, a love for people he disliked.

Applecross

APPLECROSS might be the name of a village in South Devon; we can picture the place, situated on the side of an estuary and backed by a cider orchard. Very different was the Applecross, Mouth of the Crossan River, I saw from the Stornaway steamer, as it slowed down to pick up a passenger tossing in a small boat. It was the middle of the night and, queer place, I thought, that one has to leave at such an hour. Its row of white houses gleamed so ghostly through the darkness, that when the man climbed on board I looked at him with interest; but there was nothing unusual about him and all I wondered was, which had he eaten last, his supper or his breakfast? Going back to my berth I said, Some day I must visit Applecross.

When I passed it again, I was in the same steamer, but northward bound this time and by day. Two passengers left it for the tossing boat. The village was built on much the same lines as Plockton, except that there was only one line, the row of white houses, presenting a trim appearance as they stood arm-in-arm along the shore. But the prospect was different; while Plockton, that much admired village, turning its back to the sea, looks across a small firth to the luxuriant and rocky Duncraig, Applecross gazed out on the western ocean. It gazed intently as though Raasay and the Skye mountains did not block the view. Again I said, Some day——

The occasion came when, staying at Kyle, I heard an Applecross ferry had started and I became one of its first passengers. It took me as far as Toscaig, leaving a long five miles to walk. It was the season when bluebells, tossing in the wind, were uncertain whether they were ringing out spring or ringing in summer. Indifferent to woodland shade in the moist Highland climate, they grew by the roadside; while those on my left were blue, those on my right, struck by the low western sun, were a glowing red. Iris leaves advanced from the ditches over damp meadows; the effect was of an army marching underground, but waving short Roman swords in the air and showing here and there a yellow flag. Far out at sea was Raasay with its strange hill, Dun Caan, which the natives told Boswell was higher than the Cuillin. Perhaps that was why, having climbed it, he danced on its flat summit. The flush of evening must have gone to my head like wine; I could not shake off the fancy he danced there still.

Seeing no church at Applecross, I asked where the stones were and was told that the week before a man had hunted for them all over the hills. As I imagined them well-known, that seemed odd; so I changed the question to "But where is the church?" The answer was pointed out to me on the far side of the bay. It was the north side, which St Maelrubha had no doubt chosen as the sunniest, when he established his monastery in the seventh century. There he lived for over fifty years, but only off and on, for he travelled about much, making a great name for himself, making many names in places called after him, such as Loch Maree. Perhaps that loch, at one time part of the salt-water Loch Ewe, having become separate, needed a new name, and the saint had a shrine on one of its islands. On the island was also a holy well, as there was in Mull, where Tobermory probably means Maelrubha's Well. Ashig in Skye is short for Askimilruby, Maelrubha's Ferry; near by hung from a tree a holy bell which of itself rang the canonical hours. He died in the Black Isle, but his body refused to be buried there, even to be lifted till four red-headed men came to bear it back to Applecross. Still stranger was the case of one of his successors, Abbot Ruairidh; he died in Ulster where he had sought refuge from the raiding vikings, but his body of its own accord came back on a swimming stone. After Iona Applecross is the holiest place in Scotland.

What looked like a porter, a monk in long grey cassock, stood by the graveyard gate; but it was a tall stone slab, perhaps the boat that had brought back the abbot. On one side something was carved, too weathered now for my finger to trace; if it was a foliated cross, that side contrasted strangely with the other side, so thick with lichen blowing in the wind that it was like a shaggy animal's back. It was the only ancient stone I saw, not troubling to look for others, even for the stone that marked the saint's grave. I found myself in what might have been a city cemetery, filled with expensive monuments. The holiness of the place had made it eclectic, gathering people from all parts, even distant towns. I thought of the belief that anyone who takes a handful of soil from the saint's grave can go to the ends of the earth and return safely; perhaps these sleepers had taken a handful, for all had come back safely like the abbot and the saint himself. So much of the ground sacred to them, I did not feel the place was holy.

The air was still, as I went round the bay back to the village; rushes hung listening heads, and the sea, drawing over itself a rich cover, turquoise and yellow tinged with orange, had fallen into a calm sleep. Near the shore it breathed with a gentle rise and fall, the mountains reflected on it shaking with a continuous easy earthquake. The mountains themselves, softened by the evening light, were of the same fine texture as their reflections, giving the impression they were only visible, not tangible. It was one of those evenings which occur in the Western Highlands when the scene takes on a heart-breaking beauty; it was sad, because it was beyond the mind's capacity to receive, being infinite. I thought of the man who the week before had gone over the hills looking for stones; a geologist no doubt, he understood better than I did what had gone to the making of the scene. Yet I could not rightly think he had seen what I was seeing now, an eternal world with no rocks, water, sand, grass, as these things are commonly understood. And I saw it only because it revealed itself. The correspondence was mutual, so that I thought of the woman who said at the elevation of the Host, "He looks at me and I look at Him." Unlike the cemetery it was holy, a world in which I felt both at home and a trespasser.

The Tweed

"You live in a very pretty place," said Dorothy Wordsworth to an old woman, and "Yes," she replied, "the water of Tweed is a bonny water." She might have said "beautiful," if that had been a natural word for an old Scots woman. She lived near Innerleithen, and from there down to its meeting with the Ettrick Water the Tweed has much beauty. But perhaps it is at its best when, joined by the Leader Water, it flows under steep wooded banks to Dryburgh. On Bemersyde Hill, where the road rises high above the river's horseshoe bend round Old Melrose, Scott often stood to admire his favourite view, and there, by a strange accident, his funeral procession was halted for a time. Farther down, the ruined Dryburgh Abbey with its beautiful St Mary's Aisle lies in a setting of great charm. There the funeral procession made its final halt:

The glory dies not and the grief is past.[1]

But if the woman had said "beautiful," it would not have suggested what "bonny" suggests, her warm feeling for the Tweed. She does not call it a river; she gives it a more elemental name, "a water." Rivers meant much to the people of the Border country, and they are usually so named. The name might stand for the valley through which the river flowed; people still speak of going up the Gala Water. It might even mean those who lived in the valley.

[1] Sir E. Brydges, *Sonnet on Scott's Death*.

To Jamie Telfer o' the Fair Dodhead, appealing for his help, Buccleuch cries,

> "Gar warn the water, braid and wide,
>   Gar warn it sune and hastilie,"

and he assures Jamie that Wat o' Harden and his sons will answer the call, and also

> "Wi' them will Borthwick Water ride."

For the Tweed the woman could hardly have failed to have a warm feeling; it is in itself a friendly river. You feel nothing friendly about the Tay; the longest river in Britain, it is on too majestic a scale. A rapid river like the Spey has no time for your acquaintance, and the Forth with its silver windings is too self-absorbed. But the Tweed chatters to you from its broad pebbly stretches, while it is just as human when, having slowly and cautiously approached a rocky linn, it quickens its pace and leaps into the pool, where it circles about, the bubbles gazing with a bewildered look. The Tweed so shares its changing moods with you that you hardly distinguish between yourself and the river.

There is a friendliness about the whole Border country. Its beauty is simple, due mainly to the mingling of rich cultivated valleys with benty hills and heathery moors; you get a similar contrast in the Lake District, but here the valleys are kindlier and the hills less forbidding. Words with a human connotation have often been applied to these small hills; to Dorothy Wordsworth they had "a pensive softness." The braes of Yarrow are "dowie," which means sad as when it is said of Clerk Colven,

> He's mounted on his berry-brown steed,
>   And dowie dowie rade he hame.

Lord Cockburn put it in a different way when he spoke of himself as "impressed with that peculiar feeling of softness and of sacredness which pervades all our border scenery."[1] Andrew Lang, returning from a visit to Killarney, said to his brother, "The beauty of the Irish Lakes is rather that of the Professional Beauty. When one comes back to the Border, there one finds the same beauty one used to see in the face of one's mother, or of one's old nurse." Certainly no other country has evoked a warmer feeling in its people:

> Happy the craw
> That biggs in the Trotten shaw,
> And drinks o' the Water o' Dye—
> For nae mair mae I.

No doubt Dorothy Wordsworth shared the old woman's feeling; the Tweed had, she said, "a name which has been sweet to my ears almost as far back as I can remember anything." It was endeared to her by the Border ballads. Perhaps these meant something to the woman as well, for it was from such old people that Scott obtained much of his *Minstrelsy of the Scottish Border*. One of them was the mother of Hogg, the Ettrick Shepherd, who gave him *Auld Maitland*. She at least was proud of the ballads, even grudging the publicity they had in the *Minstrelsy*; as she complained, "they were made for singing an' no for reading; an' worst o' a', they're neither right spell'd nor right setten' doun." Perhaps Dorothy's woman may have sung them in her youth, milking sheep in the early morning, for on such occasions they appear to have been sung:

> I've heard a lilting at our yowe-milking,
> Lasses a-lilting before the dawn o' day.[2]

[1] *Circuit Journeys.*   [2] Jean Elliot, *Lament for Flodden.*

I

The words would not always come trippingly off the tongue, many lines being lame on their metrical feet, somewhat like Scott himself. But they are all the better for irregularity; at least you look for it in poems which have been carelessly handed down from any time between the end of the fourteenth century and the middle of the seventeenth. But if they are halt, they are not blind. They may refer vaguely to an imaginary place,

> where the white lilies grow
> On the banks o' Italie,

but they see persons and events sharply, not like the later poet who said of Annie Laurie,

> Her neck is like the swan.

Nor are they dumb; the Border dialect is very expressive. What equivalent in English could there be to Caleb Balderstone's description of Ravenswood, "He's daft—clean daft—red wud, and awa wi 't!"?[1] Mrs Hogg said to Scott, "ye hae broken the charm o' them now"; but they still act as a charm, casting a spell over us in a way that no other kind of poetry does, a spell that somehow seems out of proportion to their real merit. They make the Tweed with its tributaries different from other rivers; we can share the woman's feeling when she said, "the water of Tweed is a bonny water."

The Tweed did not inspire the unknown poets in the magic way of the spring Hippocrene, but it was an indirect cause of inspiration. Forming with the Liddel Water a doubtful boundary between two hostile nations, it gave rise to strife, set the stage for real alarms and excursions, in which they found inspiring subjects. The Scots often

---

[1] Scott, *The Bride of Lammermoor.*

crossed the Border, in private raids or, as Shakespeare knew, in open invasion, if the English were elsewhere engaged. To King Henry V, contemplating war with France, Westmoreland points out,

> the eagle England being in prey,
> To her unguarded nest the weasel Scot
> Comes sneaking and so sucks the princely eggs.

Even Dante refers to this strife between the Scots and English.[1] But everything shows that the Scots suffered more in the end. King David I founded large abbeys, Melrose, Kelso and Jedburgh the most notable, and while we cannot doubt the piety of saintly Queen Margaret's son in doing so, it may have been with the hope that their lands would be respected as sanctuaries by the English. But a ruin like Jedburgh Abbey tells a different story. Enough remains to make it impressive, but little is left of Jedburgh Castle, where at the marriage of Alexander III, presaging his death, the dancing skeleton appeared; like Roxburgh Castle it was destroyed by the Scots themselves to prevent its further occupation by the English. The Crown gave grants of land to the Border towns in the hope that it would be in the citizens' interest to defend them; the citizens still proudly keep up their Common Ridings, but apart from a few odd buildings, such as Queen Mary's House in Jedburgh, these towns themselves are gone. We need not look for old towns in the Border country; only the names are ancient. Roxburgh, the largest of them, was never rebuilt; as it had a convent, a mint and a palace, it is a remarkable case of a town disappearing to, literally, its last stone.

So it is not surprising that the Border poetry is tragic; it is more tragic than the corresponding poetry of wild

[1] *Paradiso*, Canto XIX.

Northumberland. We see that in comparing two poems on
the same theme, the English *Three Ravens* with its mild
ending,

> God send every gentleman
> Such hounds, such hawks, and such a leman!

and the Scottish *Twa Corbies* with its stark ending,

> O'er his white banes, when they are bare,
> The wind sall blaw for evermair.

We might be at a loss to find anything in English poetry
that equals in simple pathos *The Lament of the Border
Widow*:

> I took his body on my back,
> And whiles I gaed, and whiles I sat;
> I digg'd a grave, and laid him in,
> And happ'd him with the sod sae green.

> But think na ye my heart was sair,
> When I laid the moul' on his yellow hair;
> O think na ye my heart was wae,
> When I turn'd about, away to gae?

The picture of the woman staggering under her burden and
laying it down at times to sit and rest might haunt us
many days.

Scott seems to have found most of his ballads in Liddesdale, which lies farther south than the Tweed, a country so
wild and remote that Lockhart says the first wheeled
carriage to travel through it was Scott's gig. With its
peculiar position it hardly admitted its allegiance to the
Crown; of Johnny Armstrong King James V asks,

> "What needs that knave that a king should have,
> But the sword of honour and the crown!"

Its lairds might be hand in glove with the lairds of Redesdale or North Tynedale in Northumberland. After Queen Mary's flight into England they became so bold that a punitive army was sent against them from Edinburgh. Its commander said, "When once I unsheath my sword I will leave no peel, bastel or onstead standing from end to end of your sweet valley," and it is believed that no house was left standing. But more often the raids were carried into England:

> The outlaws come frae Liddesdale,
> They herry Redesdale far and near;
> The rich man's gelding it maun gang,
> They canna pass the puir man's mare.

Hereabouts originated the word "blackmail," which meant money a farmer paid to a laird for his protection; when Jamie Telfer sought Gibby Elliot's help, he replied,

> "Gae seek your succour where ye paid black-mail,
> For, man! ye ne'er paid money to me."

Westburnflat reflects back the spirit of Liddesdale when he says, "thae were gude days on the Border when there was neither peace nor justice heard of";[1] and it survives in Hobbie Elliot when he arranges to fight out his quarrel with Dick Turnbull at Jeddart on the Rood-day because, as he says, "that's like a thing settled in a peaceable way!" So it is not surprising to find at the heart of Liddesdale the strangest of all castles, called after a hermit's cell, Hermitage. There is nothing very remarkable about the building; it is not as striking as Neidpath Castle on the Tweed, a stark symbol of old warfare, yet admirable in its proportions. But it has a spiritual quality, a suggestion of evil

[1] Scott, *The Black Dwarf.*

that mocks its pious name. Whoever owned it, from Lord Soulis to Bothwell, the overlord was an imp of Satan, named Redcap. So black was its reputation that people thought it was gradually sinking under the weight of its iniquity.

But for the best ballads we have to return to the Tweed and the waters that feed it, especially the Yarrow, which unites with the Ettrick Water below Carterhaugh, where the Queen of the Fairies carried off young Tamlin. The Yarrow flows finely among rocks and trees under the braes of Harewood, but otherwise it has little of the striking beauty of the Jed Water, as it runs for some miles by the rose-coloured cliffs above Jedburgh. But it has songs and ballads, which make Wordsworth's question,

> What's Yarrow but a river bare?

merely rhetorical. These have given it a fame that draws crowds on a fine day. One wet day, when I was there, I was set on, almost pushed over, by sheep; I was amazed, till I remembered seeing sheep run to be fed with bread by picnickers at the Grey Mare's Tail. But Yarrow pleads to retain its quiet and solitude; more than any other part of the Border country it impresses you with "that peculiar feeling of softness and of sacredness." Its houms are dowie, and a crowd intrudes on their sorrow. Perhaps they borrow their dowieness from the songs and ballads, which are always tragic:

> "Hold up, hold up, Lord William," she says,
>   "For I fear that ye are slain"—
> "'Tis naething but the shadow o' my scarlet cloak,
>   That shines in the water sae plain."

But in the Border poetry we seldom get away from sadness, except when we pass into Elfland, as in *Young Tamlin* and

Thomas the Rhymer, two ballads which can hold up their heads in the very best poetic company. In Elfland Thomas the Rhymer spent seven pleasant years; his only misfortune was that the Queen gave him an apple to eat which compelled him to speak the truth:

> "My tongue is my ain," true Thomas he said;
> "A gudely gift ye wad gie to me!
> I neither dought to buy or sell
> At fair or tryst where I might be."

Yet even in Elfland he was not far away from such things as the shadow of Lord William's bloody cloak:

> For a' the blude that's shed on the earth
> Rins through the springs o' that countrie.

The Findhorn

"You may well look at it; see what it has done to my house." I turned from the river to where she pointed; one side of the house had been swept away. "The flood of last summer," she explained, and added, "Water is worse than fire." Dante could not have said anything more graphic; I could see the raging torrent, gnawing at the stones, but petrifying the woman. She was powerless to fight against it as Achilles was against the river-god, Scamander. Looking back at the river I shook a reproachful head. I felt some responsibility for its conduct, for we belong to the same county, Morayshire, though the Findhorn only by adoption.

Old travellers, who are free from modern sophistications, have given no other county higher praise. "The delectable planure of Murray, a second Lombardy," says William Lithgow, and John Macky, "one of the beautifullest counties in Britain; the Vale of Evesham is not comparable to it." They might have said more if they had gone a little out of their way to explore the Findhorn, for that river is its chief adornment. "I hold the Findhorn to be indisputably the finest river for scenery in Britain," is the summing up of a judge, Lord Cockburn.[1] Yet unlike the Wye and the Dove it has no great fame. Each season thousands of tourists cross the Suspension Bridge near Forres in their eager quest for scenic views of the High-

[1] *Circuit Journeys.*

lands, but few turn aside or give a thought to a river of which Charles St John says, "I do not know a stream that more completely realizes all one's ideas of the beauty of Highland scenery."[1]

If the Findhorn could have achieved fame by flooding, it would have done so in the first week of August 1829, the date of the Great Flood. It was heralded by a remarkable display of Northern Lights, and of the preliminary rain Geikie says, "the downpour does not seem to have been equalled within historic times." The current was so swift that for Sir Thomas Dick Lauder "it was scarcely possible to follow with the eye the trees that floated like straws on its surface."[2] Huge banks fell away; of one about a hundred feet high a farmer told him that it fell "wi' a sort o' a dumb sound." The water rose to an astonishing height in the gorges; one of his gardeners caught "*a fine salmon, at an elevation of 50 feet above the ordinary level of the Findhorn.*" He caught it, not with a rod, but with an umbrella. The brothers, John Sobieski and Charles Edward Stuart, who had just come to reside at Logie House, saw the water at the same height: "When dawn broke, it appeared sweeping through the trees, which the evening before hung fifty feet above its bank."[3] The river, as though in compensation for two lives lost, resurrected the body of a red-haired man. It made a strange choice, for the man had a rope round his neck, the rope with which he had hanged himself and been buried.

A waterfall might have brought fame to the Findhorn; but that is not certain, for few know the name of the river with the grandest waterfall in Britain, the Falls of Glo-

[1] *Wild Sports of the Highlands.*
[2] *An Account of the Great Floods of August 1829.*
[3] *Lays of the Deer Forest.*

mach. One or two towns on its banks, such as Grantown-on-Spey, would have made it well known; but people kept their habitations away from so excitable a river, liable at any time to overstep the mark; to have built a house on its rocky bank would have been to build it on sand. Perhaps a poet might have brought it fame. The Findhorn has not been without its poets; there was Henry Mackenzie, the Man of Feeling, who lived at Coulmony House and wandered about its woods, attaching poems to trees. Though he invoked the Spirits who haunted the place,

> Simplicity, whose brows adorn
> The daisies washed by dewy morn;
> And Pity, with a lambkin pressed,
> A dying lambkin, to her breast,

somehow his poems never won for him a fame the river might have shared. And there were the brothers, John Sobieski and Charles Edward Stuart. They show a poetic feeling for the Findhorn in a note to *Lays of the Deer Forest*: "Although it has pleased some of the noble learned to personify the Findhorn as a *masculine* deity, it should be known that '*she*' is a feminine person—a water-nymph." The elder brother wrote a poem, *To the Findhorn*, in which he tells her that if he shares the fate of his royal father he will spread his wan and wasted arms to the gleam that warms her bank. The younger brother wrote one *To the Divie*, a tributary, in which he says very truly,

> Thou wilt not be less bright and clear,
> Though I have stained thee with a tear.

But it is not in poetry the brothers have achieved their fame but in fiction, the claim that they were the sons of Prince Charles Edward, the Young Pretender, a claim which greatly astonished their father, a man named Allen.

An open valley would have gained for the Findhorn more publicity. The Wye and the Dove invite you to their side; you can drive down the Wye Valley and walk down Dovedale; but the Findhorn swirling round high dangerous rocks gives no gushing welcome. Yet there are places where it is accessible enough. At Relugas you need walk only a hundred yards from the road to test the truth of Charles St John's exclamation, "Surely there is no other river in the world so beautiful!" At Dulsie Bridge you need not leave the road to answer for yourself his question, "What spot in the world can excel in beauty the landscape?" How strange this river has not been more admired. The water-nymph might be indignant that her charms are so slighted. Might she not show her indignation, or at least call attention to herself, by an occasional flood? But I thought of the woman's house with the broken side, clearly the work of a water-kelpie. That idea about the water-nymph would not hold water.

The Immortal Memory

CAPTAIN TOPHAM was surprised by the Edinburgh flats, the ground-floor flat the cheapest, the rent rising as you climbed the narrow stair; it was different in London. From a room in a low flat, shared with a friend, cheap because close to the famous night smells, Robert Burns issued to visit the city's gentry and *literati*. "Who were they? Men like myself. Besides I have two good pairs of breeks. So hey, brave Robin lad, cock up your beaver." Clad in his buckskin breeches he was not afraid to face the Duchess of Gordon. Henry Mackenzie, author of his favourite book, *The Man of Feeling*, had hailed him as "the Heaven-taught ploughman." He was not a ploughman, but a farmer; yet it was as well to play that rôle. It was at the plough the Muse had cast over him her inspiring mantle, as it was also at the plough Elijah had cast his mantle over Elisha. The mantle was all that mattered; he would be content with his brose and kail,

> As lang's the Muses dinna fail
> To say the grace.

And the Tuneful Sisters had not been saying it in vain. The city—

> Edina! Scotia's darling seat!—

had accepted him; he was, in fact, "in a fair way of becoming as eminent as Thomas à Kempis or John Bunyan."

The comparison with these writers, as also with Elisha, is not to be pressed. The poems which had so delighted the Ayrshire folk, among whom they had been widely distributed, the "priest-skelping" poems, he thought it wise to leave out of the Kilmarnock Edition; most of them appeared in the Edinburgh Edition, but *Holy Willie's Prayer* was published late and anonymously, while *The Jolly Beggars* he professed he had forgotten he ever wrote. But no one could say he was not a religious poet. If he wrote in church about the Louse he saw on a Lady's Bonnet, the poem turned out to be as good as a sermon:

> O wad some Power the giftie gie us
> To see oursels as ithers see us!

And there was *The Cotter's Saturday Night* with its moving picture of the traditional family worship. It was not only pious, but also patriotic:

> From scenes like these, old Scotia's grandeur springs.

Anything about Scotland was gratifying. The Union of Parliaments in 1707 had made Scotland seem a minor country, but it was not, as Seafield said, "the end of an auld sang." David Hume had won a European reputation, overshadowing the English philosophers. And now a new hope for poetry appeared in the "Heaven-taught ploughman." Some of the *literati* might not have joined the Freemasons in their toast, "Caledonia's Bard, brother Burns"; he was shrewd enough himself to realise it might be due to "the honest prejudice of Scotsmen." Yet it was to prove a very small prelude to the toast, "the Immortal Memory." To no other memory have so many glasses been raised.

"Caledonia's Bard"! Burns had been regarding himself

as only Coila's. Genius of Kyle, she had appeared to him in a *Vision*, addressing him in verse, poor perhaps for a Muse,

> "All hail! my own inspirèd bard!
> In me thy native Muse regard,"

and crowning him with holly, not the most comfortable coronal. She was clad in a large green mantle, which was nothing less than the land itself with its mountains and rivers; yet she contrived to show through it a leg,

> An' such a leg! my bonie Jean
> Only could peer it.

This amorous display may suggest a mutual affection. Certainly he had a strong feeling for his "dear native country, the ancient Baileries of Carrick, Kyle and Cunningham." He watched with a fatherly fondness the wee burns trot or toddle down a hill, while for the large rivers he had a great respect; inspired by Coila, he would make them as famous as

> Th' Illisus, Tiber, Thames, an' Seine.

With the Doon at least he has more or less succeeded, for there, FitzGerald tells us,[1] Tennyson broke into a passion of tears. But he has made famous much more than Ayrshire's rivers. In a way this has furthered his own fame, for thousands of people who have not read his poems, driving past Mossgiel, have pointed out to them the field where his coulter destroyed the house of a fellow-mortal, the *Mouse*, and also uprooted that mysterious plant, the *Mountain Daisy*. Arriving at Mauchline, they view the scene of the *Jolly Beggars* and the *Holy Fair*. And the characters are still there: Black Geordie Gibson with his wife, Poosie

---

[1] *Euphranor*.

Nansie, and his daughter, that Atalanta, Racer Jess, Holy Willie and Daddy Auld, with others such as Robert Wilson, the Gallant Weaver, and James Humphrey, the Bleth'rin Bitch, they are all there in the churchyard.

Strong drink went easily to Burns's head, for he was no toper; fame went less easily, for he was no fool. He was shrewd enough to suspect, "Novelty may attract the attention of mankind a while; to it I may owe my present éclat." In his depressed moods, caused by the heart trouble that in the end proved fatal, he even foresaw failure: "I look down on the future as I would into the bottomless pit." Certainly he was doing little to add to his éclat; the Edinburgh Edition, which had followed the Kilmarnock, was having no sequel. But there came a happy day! Mrs Burns had lately made him the present of a fine boy; she was getting stout again and at breakfast laid about her as lustily as a Reaper from the corn-ridge. Perhaps too long a wait for dinner that day sent her out to look for her husband. She related how she found him on his favourite path by the Nith. "He was busily crooning to himself, so that I loitered behind with the little ones among the broom. He presently began reciting as if agonised with joy. He was reciting very loud with tears rolling down his cheeks a poem which he had only begun that morning, a poem to be called Tam o' Shanter." Pleased with the poem, Burns compared it with the fine boy: each was his *chef d'œuvre* in its species of manufacture, and both showed in his opinion a force of genius which he despaired of ever excelling. Though the poem was written in Dumfriesshire, the scene is in Kyle, and Coila has not failed the sightseers. Few buildings in Scotland are better known than Alloway Kirk and the Auld Brig o' Doon. Even subsidiary spots are noted;

> the thorn, aboon the well,
> Where Mungo's mither hang'd hersel',

or at least the well, can be inspected, perhaps with wonder why the mother of St Mungo, the patron saint of Glasgow Cathedral, should have hanged herself on a thorn. Written in one day, *Tam o' Shanter* has been described as "the best day's work ever done in Scotland."

Burns redrafted many of his *Letters* and kept copies, as though foreseeing that on them his fame would in part depend. He may not have attached the same importance to his *Songs*, most of them written in his later, even declining, years, and contributed to song-collections, often unsigned. The world's most famous song, *Auld Lang Syne*, was published anonymously. He wrote the greater number in English, as he was advised, a help to their popularity, but he insisted in giving them "a sprinkling of our native tongue." This sprinkling gives them a flavour, which we should miss.

> Scots, who have with Wallace bled,

the line, lacking that flavour, is insipid; it makes English by itself seem a poor language. Patriotic, convivial, sentimental, amorous, suiting every taste, the *Songs* have sung their way to people's hearts. Without them it is doubtful if a Glasgow library would contain more than 3,500 books about Robert Burns.

Burns pointed out to his friend, William Simson, the way to become a poet, as it had been pointed out to himself by Coila:

> The muse, nae poet ever fand her,
> Till by himsel he learn'd to wander,
> Adown some trottin burn's meander,
>   An' no think lang.

But when he went on,

> O sweet to stray, an' pensive ponder
>   A heart-felt sang!

he made it clear it was not Nature's charms he found inspiring. The Ayrshire scene, though attractive, had not the sublimity he saw in a woman, perhaps in her figure no less than in her face. What he felt about her he describes: "I look on the sex with something like the admiration with which I regard the starry sky in a frosty December night." Coila had appeared to him in a *Vision*, but he needed no supernatural inspiration. "Do you imagine I fast and pray for the celestial emanation? Tout au contraire! I have a glorious recipe; I put myself on a regimen of admiring a fine woman." So Nature served him for little more than the background to an affecting scene.

> Ayr, gurgling, kiss'd his pebbled shore,
>   O'erhung with wild-woods, thickening green;
> The fragrant birch and hawthorn hoar,
>   Twin'd amorous round the raptur'd scene.

As a condensed description of trees putting out their leaves "thickening green" could not be bettered, but "amorous" and "raptur'd" show the wood is there less for its own sake than for its sentimental value. But Coila should not grudge he has used her landscape in such a way. After all he has adorned it with all manner of monuments, inscribed stones, pillars, statues, towers, and even a Greek temple. Burns's fame is solid in Ayrshire.

But the fame of Burns is not local; his poems have been translated into most European languages, including Flemish and Gaelic. The Russians are fortunate in having a translation by their poet Marshak; perhaps others are less fortunate.

K

O my Luve's like a red, red rose:

usually the line is translated with only one "red," though its whole beauty lies in the "red, red."

Ca' the yowes to the knowes:

the line seems to miss something in the French translation,

Appelle les brebis sur les hauteurs:

and from the inspiring line,

Sing hey, my braw John Highlandman,

the flavour seems lost in the Italian,

Cantate, oh! il mio bravo Giovanni il Montanaro!

As for the Latin

Commilites Wallacio,

it does not even look like a translation of the line,

Scots, wha hae wi' Wallace bled.

His poems have also been translated into Asiatic languages, such as Hindustani and Chinese, so that his fame is world-wide. Goethe called him a great poet, thinking of his *Songs*. If he is not a great poet, he is all the more one of the world's wonders.

The Speyside Ladies

As I peered through a window of the derelict house, I almost hoped to see the ghost of that deceased lady, Mrs Smith. But that was foolish; for all I knew, she might have died in India, where she married and settled down. If she haunts the house, the Doune, and its neighbourhood, Rothiemurchus Forest, it is under her maiden name, Elizabeth Grant, and only in the pages of her book, *Memoirs of a Highland Lady*.

Rothiemurchus Forest is one of the surviving parts of the ancient Wood of Caledon. Its trees are mostly Scots pines, their red athletic boughs gleaming through the bottle-green foliage. Being self-sown, they are not regimented as in a modern forest, but straggle through heather, juniper and birch like a defeated army. "The whole lay in the bosom of the Grampians, in a bend of a bow, as it were, formed by the mountains, the Spey being the string and our boundary." By the Grampians Elizabeth Grant means the Cairngorms, mountains of which Taylor, the Water-poet, rightly said that between them and the London hills, Shooter's and Highgate, there was no comparison. Viewed from Rothiemurchus, they rise from tumbled foot-hills forming an enormous wall that might be guarding heaven; certainly it hides a large part of the sky; most formidable in winter when, covered with snow, the mountains become their own ghosts. It would not occur to Elizabeth Grant to climb them; she might have said what Bailie Nicol Jarvie said of lesser heights about Aberfoyle, "it wad tire the very deevil's wings to flee to the tap o' them"; only, a refined Highland lady, she did not speak like the Bailie and his friends, "bits o' Glasgow bodies."

But we can follow her through the Forest, "wandering on among the immense roots of trees, and scattering to gather cranberries," that is, if we can keep up with her pony. We can follow her to Loch-an-Eilean and watch what we cannot now see, the osprey or fishing-eagle that nests in the ruined island stronghold; or we can follow her farther, to the wildest loch on the Scottish mainland, Loch Einich, from which rises to 2,000 feet the precipitous Sgoran Dubh. Loch Morlich is more beautiful, lying below Cairngorm, a mountain that gives its name to its neighbours and to a rock-crystal; but we cannot follow her there, for it never seems to have called to her, "Come unto these yellow sands." That may have been because it lay outside her father's estate, in Glenmore Forest. But on the mountain itself her eyes must often have rested, though perhaps not noticing with the Ettrick Shepherd how

> his mighty form
> Disturbs the moon in passing by,
> And smiles above the thunder storm.

But wherever we follow her, "at every step there lies a picture." She had no gift of poetic description, "I am not given to poetry generally," she says, and we can believe it from her disparaging account of a poet she met in London: "that poor, mad poet Coleridge, who never held his tongue, stood pouring out a deluge of words meaning nothing, with eyes on fire, and his silver hair streaming down to his waist." Yet she is communicative enough to make us share her delight in what she sees and, generally, her feeling for the Highlands. Queen Victoria had the same gift of communication if she could say, "Lord Aberdeen was quite touched when I told him I was so attached to the dear, dear Highlands."

Elizabeth Grant mentions in her *Memoirs* a John Peter Grant of Laggan as "the only surviving child of nineteen born to the minister and his celebrated wife." One wonders how the wife, Mrs Grant of Laggan, found time to produce that other offspring which made her celebrated and still survives, *Letters from the Mountains in Three Volumes*. Her husband was not only minister of Laggan, but a farmer as well; "we have taken up our refuge in the pastor's cottage, which is literally pastoral," she says, meaning that the manse is also a farm-house. There she baked her bread, brewed her ale, and spun her flax and wool. And she received many visitors, welcoming them to a warm corner in her cottage and in her heart, hoping that the warmth of the welcome would atone for the coldness of the mountain air. There may have been more occasions than one on which this busy lady said, "I bless the closing shades of evening, and am much tempted to kiss my hand to the moon, as she walks in her brightness," a temptation which came also to the patient Job. But she had a consolation: "I frankly own that the exercise of this rhyming faculty does now and then cheer the gloom of care." She admits that "to attempt composition under the restraints of prudential reserves is, to use an elegant simile, like running a race in boots"; yet, as she says, "such races have been run and such poems have been written."

The "pastor's cottage" looked over a flat meadow to the Upper Spey where, nowadays, having suffered the double indignity of being narrowed to a canal and then broadened to a reservoir, it begins to pick up its customary

good spirits. But Mrs Grant had more feeling for a tributary, the Bronnach, that, passing close to the house, was
almost a member of the household. It was an unruly member in winter, brawling like a termagant, but at other times
it could speak with so plaintive a voice that she was
tempted to ask what ailed it. The district is wild and
mountainous. Defoe had a poor opinion of it: "call'd
Loquabre, it is indeed a frightful Country full of hidious
desart Mountains." Mrs Grant speaks of their sublime
solitude, from which we wish to look down on low pursuits;
but from her curious description of them, "there are no
first floors at all, but all is cellar, or garret," one imagines
she climbed them only in flights of fancy, flying from base
to summit. But at least she had crossed them by the Pass of
Corrieyarrick on visits to Fort Augustus, a road having
been constructed by General Wade, whose name occurs in
maps and in an old version of the National Anthem. After
their return from America she had lived with her father,
an army officer, at Fort Augustus, a small town that by its
situation reminded her of New York. It made her poetical,
for of the barracks she wrote, "it is so fancifully planted
round with the mountain-ash, you would think Vertumnus
commanded here, and had garrisoned the fort with Dryads."
She is more her natural self when she is nearer home and
sees how the Bronnach, having reached the flat meadow,
"circles round so often, that it seems inclined to revisit its
source." Unfortunately the *Letters* contain only two or
three of her poems, and they might not be her best; they
might even be her worst.

These Speyside ladies relate things that make the people
of their time seem far away. There was the case of old
George Ross, husband of the Rothiemurchus hen-wife. He
caught a chill, and inflammation came on which a bottle of

whisky, and even more, failed to cure. Friends gathered to wake him in the old fashion, shaved and partly dressed and set up in bed. After refreshments had gone round, they took to dancing and so shook the floor that the body tumbled out of bed in the middle of a reel. Imagining old George had come to life again, they fled shrieking, but afterwards they regarded it as a warning to the hen-wife, for whatever she had been to the hens, she had been an unpleasant wife to her husband.

But if the people seem far away, so also do the Highlands they knew. Both ladies noted the beginning of a change which they did not welcome. Passing through Killiecrankie Elizabeth Grant thought it still beautiful, but not as on a former journey, "for no Perth traders had built their villas on its sheltered banks." Mrs Grant did not favour the new roads into a country where every house had its musician and every hamlet its poet. Now her new roads are the old ones, many of them under the water of raised lochs. The natural lines of road, river and loch have been altered, and they are hard lines for one who remembers them as they were. Roads may have opened up the Highlands, but not the Highlands of the Speyside ladies, or even of Queen Victoria and myself.

The Two Shepherds

THERE are two statues of James Hogg, the Ettrick Shepherd. One is in Ettrickdale, on the site of the two-roomed cottage in which he was born, strangely called Ettrick Hall; it stands close to the road so that the Shepherd can see all who come to visit his grave. His body lies in the near-by churchyard, and next to him lies his maternal grandfather, Will o' Phaup, commended on his tombstone for his "feats of frolic." The other statue is only a few miles away, in Yarrow. A plaided figure, seated on an eminence with his dog Hector, the Shepherd looks down on the head of St Mary's Loch, perhaps not without a sidelong glance at Tibbie Shiel's Inn. He might be recalling, "O happy days, that I have lain on the green hill-side, with my plaid around me, best mantle of inspiration, my faithful Hector sitting like a very Christian by my side, bonny St Mary's Loch lying like a smile below." That there should be these two statues in Ettrick Forest, both of a supernatural size, suggests that the Ettrick Shepherd was a poet of some magnitude. But a truer explanation might be that there were two Shepherds, who combined to make a great impression on their own generation and the next. One was real, the Shepherd who herded sheep in the Forest and wrote poems, the other more or less imaginary, the Shepherd who ate oysters and discoursed in John Wilson's *Noctes Ambrosianae*. The second attached itself to the first like a gigantic shadow cast by the evening sun, gigantic, indeed, if Professor Ferrier, Wilson's son-in-law and editor, is right in saying, "in wisdom the Shepherd equals the Socrates of Plato; in humour the Falstaff of Shakespeare."

James Hogg was a real shepherd to his readers, the more welcome because they were tired of artificial shepherds, the Corydons and Damons of the pastoral poets. They were well supplied with information about him, for he attached three autobiographical sketches to his books, and published a fourth in the *Scots Magazine*. He began his career at the age of seven by herding cows, his half-yearly wage being a ewe lamb and a pair of shoes. After a short interval when he attended school he went back to herding cows till such time as he was fit to don the shepherd's plaid and herd a flock of sheep. It was when he had driven sheep into Edinburgh for sale, and was irked by the delay in selling them, that he arranged for the printing of his first book of poems, *Scottish Pastorals*. His readers knew of his want of education; his attendance at school had lasted less than six months, so that he could speak of himself as one "who could neither write nor read with accuracy when twenty"; it may have increased their admiration for his poems. He could have done more to educate himself; John Leyden, his fellow-poet, also born in a remote shepherd's cottage, had so educated himself "that he had, before he attained his nineteenth year, confounded the doctors of Edinburgh by the portentous mass of his acquisitions in almost every department of learning."[1] But Hogg according to his friend Gillies was afraid of reading too much; it might affect his originality as a poet.

But Hogg was more than a shepherd, an Ettrick shepherd.

[1] Lockhart, *Life of Scott*.

Ettricke Forest is a fair foreste,

says one of the ballads, but the ballads themselves have
helped to make it seem so fair. You would need to cross the
moors and go down entrancing Eskdale to Gilnockie and
Canobie to find a land that for ballads equals the Forest.
Yarrow is famous for its "dowie dens," though no one
knows what the dens are. St Mary's Kirk, that gave its
name to St Mary's Loch, is the closing scene of *The
Douglas Tragedy* and *The Gay Goss Hawk*. And there is
The Young Tamlane; from Carterhaugh, "where Ettrick
and Yarrow come rushing into each other's arms," he was
carried away by the fairies. Scott tells of a man who, falling
asleep near Carterhaugh, woke to find himself in Glasgow;
that he had been carried through the air was clear when his
bonnet was found next morning hanging on Lanark church
steeple. Young Tamlane was carried to a very different
place, Fairyland; that was why, a boy "just turned of nine,"
he never grew up:

> She hadna pu'd a red red rose,
> A rose but barely three,
> Till up and starts a wee wee man
> At Lady Janet's knee.

In Hogg's time the fairies were gone; Will o' Phaup
was the last man to see and converse with the fairies, and
he had died when his grandson was a boy of five. But there
remained

The warlock men and the weird wemyng.

A farmer told Hogg how he had fired at a pair of moor-
fowl, wounding the hen, and when he went to where she
had fallen on the other side of a dyke, he found Nell ——,
picking shot out of her body. "He was extremely vexed

that he had not shot the cock, for he was almost certain he was no other than *Willie Grieve!*" It is strange Hogg should have claimed that among his female forebears were several witches, especially as no one would have doubted the claim, for, he says, "Never was the existence of witches more firmly believed in, than by the inhabitants of the mountains of Ettrick Forest at the present day." Born in the Forest and brought up by a mother who was daughter of Will o' Phaup and supplied Scott with ballads, it is not surprising Hogg aspired to be "King of the Mountain and Fairy School of poetry."

When Mrs Izett, with whom he was staying at Kinnaird House in Atholl, led Hogg into a room provided with writing materials and pointed to the river Tay as a suitable subject for a poem, he replied that a purely descriptive poem might prove dull and heavy, "though," he added, "I consider myself exquisite at descriptions of nature, and mountain scenery in particular." Perhaps his best description is of a mountain tarn; it is so calm,

> that vision scarcely could discern
> The water from the land, hazel and rock
> From their fair copies on the element,
> The shadow from the substance—save that one
> Was softer and more delicately green.

But the description is from a book of parodies, *Poetic Mirror*. Hogg is parodying Wordsworth, trying to look through his eyes and doing it well. Yet it is doubtful if he cared much for mountain tarns; Hartley Coleridge tells that when Wordsworth, conducting him round the Rydal district, said, "I'll just show you another lake, and then we'll go homewards," Hogg replied, "I dinna want to see ony mair dubs; let's step into the public." But there is no doubt about his feeling for the Forest; "Living for years in the solitude, he unconsciously formed friendships with the springs, the brooks, the caves, the hills, even with all the more fleeting and faithless pageantry of the sky," Wilson wrote in *Blackwood*. But a friend of the Lake Poets, or, as Hogg called them, the Pond Poets, Wilson had not a high opinion of the Shepherd's descriptions of scenery; he was too fond of comparing the beauties of Nature with the beauties of the lasses; it was when he turned away from Nature that the Shepherd excelled. "Whenever he treats of fairy-land, his language insensibly becomes, as it were, soft, wild, and aerial; he is the poet-laureate of the Court of Faery."

He was thinking, of course, of *Kilmeny*, written in a language peculiarly its own:

> Bonnie Kilmeny gaed up the glen;
> But it was not to meet Duneira's men,
> Nor the rosy monk of the isle to see,
> For Kilmeny was pure as pure could be.

It has an ethereal quality that tells us she is going

> where cock never crew,
> Where rain never fell, and the wind never blew.

Where this "far countrie" is we do not inquire, recognising that it has no location;

> The land of vision, it would seem,
> A still, an everlasting dream.

Kilmeny has an innocent childlike acceptance of the supernatural that makes it contrast strangely with that *diablerie*, in which the supernatural startles you with stage effects, *The Confessions of a Justified Sinner*. But it contrasts almost as much with a companion poem in *The Queen's*

Wake, a ballad, supernatural enough, yet gross and comic, *The Witch of Fife*. When the witch met the wee wee man on the Lomond Hills,

> His face was wan like the collifloure,
> For he nouthir had blude nor bane;

and when she was flying home from Carlisle after a night spent in drinking the bishop's wine, huntsmen on the Braid Hills shot at her for a bird, perhaps a moor-fowl,

> Till purpil fell the mornyng dew
> Wi' witch-blude rank and reide.

The witch and the wee wee man may have belonged to Fife, but they had relations in Ettrick Forest.

The Queen's Wake caused an immense sensation; it woke a curiosity about the Shepherd which too often could not be satisfied without a visit to his Ettrick farm. He told Lockhart that sometimes he had as many as thirty visitors in a day. Scott heard unfavourable reports about his sheep-farming. The farm, named Altrive Lake after a small burn, was a long way from a town and visitors had to be entertained. Wilson, fishing in Yarrow, wrote home to his wife that he found Hogg bottling whisky. No doubt he had something to bottle it from, "as good as a sma' still"; but there was also the food. According to Lockhart's account "a warm and hospitable disposition, so often stirred by vanity less pardonable than his, made him convert his cottage into an unpaid hostelrie for the reception of endless troups of thoughtless admirers." Or as a maid in his service reported, "it's maist awfu'; the hoose is just like a public, but wi' nae siller comen in!" His friend Gillies says that in order to get away from people and concentrate on poetic composition he left the country and went to Edinburgh.

There with his shepherd's plaid and country ways and
manner of speech, his jovial habits, quaint humour and
childlike vanity, he became an attraction apart from his
poetry. Dining with Lockhart, Crabbe was much amused
by Hogg "calling for a can of ale, while champagne and
claret, and other choice wines, were in full circulation."[1]
Yet Hogg would have denied he could not appreciate good
wine, for, asked in London if he liked champagne, he said,
"I like it fine, it's sae like ginger beer." Perhaps Lady
Williamson also was amused when he dined at her table;
invited to partake of a certain dish, he replied, "Am no
sure. Will ony body tell me what it is? I ne'er saw the like
o't." But the whole country was amused and excited by the
Shepherd as he made a magnified appearance in *Blackwood's
Magazine*. Wilson himself appeared there in a magnified
form as Christopher North, but he admitted that Bucolic
Jamie was the heart and soul of *Noctes Ambrosianae*,
articles suitably named, you might think, though the
Noctes are called *Ambrosianae* after Mr Ambrose, host of
Oman's Hotel in Edinburgh.

In a letter to Grieve, who had been Hogg's friend,
Wilson said, "I wrote the *Noctes* to benefit and do honour
to Mr Hogg, much more than to benefit myself; and but
for them, he with all his extraordinary powers would not
have been so universally admired as he now is." Yet Hogg
himself was not wholly grateful for the honour or ap-
preciative of the benefit. No doubt he approved of some of
the opinions he expressed as the Shepherd in the *Noctes*:
"Me and Wordsworth are aboon the age we live in; it's
no worthy o' us"; and he enjoyed hearing himself talk so
poetically about the Rainbow: "Is she not the Lady o'
Licht, the Queen o' Colour, the Princess o' Prisms, the

[1] *Life, by his Son.*

Heiress Apparent o' Air, and her Royal Highness of Heaven?" Having written better than anyone else about the Fairies, he could rightly say, "I've seen scores o' them, baith drunk and sober." If at times he grew convivial— "Eh? Say you the Glenlivet smells like violets? It does that, a perfect nosegay"—he was convivial in the company of the Professor of Moral Philosophy at Edinburgh University, Christopher North, alias John Wilson. But when a critic in the *Quarterly Review* called the Shepherd "a boozing buffoon," he wondered if Wilson was not treating him with too little respect. He became troubled by his appearance in the *Noctes*, frightened by the gigantic shadow cast by the midnight sun. So there were times when he grumbled and complained to Blackwood; but at another time he could write to him about Wilson, "He's my own dear John. You may assure him that

> I like my Jacky's gray breeks
> For a' the ill he's done me yet."

It was well he did like them, if only because Wilson was right in telling Grieve that without the *Noctes* Hogg would not have been so universally known as he was, for, he added, "poetical fame is fleeting and precarious."

Young Wordsworth

HE was of a stiff, moody and violent temper, the one child out of five about whose future his mother felt anxious. He once took a foil in his hand to kill himself, but his heart failed. In the large uncarpeted drawing-room, where they were playing with tops, he challenged his brother to slash with his whip an ancestral portrait; when his brother refused, "Then here goes," he said, and struck his whip through a lady's hooped petticoat. He was properly punished, but so perverse was he that he did not mind being punished. This young wretch, that Wordsworth confesses he was, is strangely unlike the growing Boy of the *Immortality Ode*. He has come into the world trailing clouds of glory; shades of the prison-house may be beginning to close about him,

> But He beholds the light, and whence it flows,
> He sees it in his joy.

One thing, however, they appear to have in common is a sense of the numinous; we read of two occasions when this was awakened in the schoolboy, both in connexion with theft. Perhaps we should not blame a boy for setting springes for woodcock; Shakespeare's painful references to traps, lime, nets, decoys and what not, are probably reminiscent of his boyhood activities. Young Wordsworth's offence was that he stole birds from other boys' springes. What happened after one theft was alarming:

> I heard among the solitary hills
> Low breathings coming after me, and sounds
> Of undistinguishable motion, steps
> Almost as silent as the turf they trod.

The other occasion was only a temporary theft. Staying a night at Patterdale on his way home for the holidays, he borrowed a boat and rowed out on the lake. Again he had the sense of being followed; St Sunday's Crag

> Towered up between me and the stars, and still,
> For so it seemed, with purpose of its own
> And measured motion like a living thing,
> Strode after me.

It was with such a sense of the numinous that men offered sacrifices to the Nature Deities, as when the pious Aeneas offered a lamb to the Tempests.

But young Wordsworth was not always in mischief; what could be more harmless than to take the dog for a walk and compose a poem? Usually he walked round Esthwaite Water, which was near his Hawkshead school. This small lake lies among low hills, with distant mountains peeping over their backs, though there is little more to satisfy their curiosity than a pleasant sheet of water. The composition of a poem flung him into a state of agitation, but the wise dog trotted on ahead and on anyone's approach ran back

> To give me timely notice, and straightway,
> Grateful for that admonishment, I hushed
> My voice, composed my gait.

The dog had its reward, for when some lovely Image,

> Full-formed, like Venus rising from the sea,

rose in the poet's mind, it was his turn to run to the dog

L

and give it a "stormy caress." When he thought of the line,
afterwards repeated in a sonnet,

> The unimaginable touch of time,

he may have felt a gentle stroke was more appropriate.
Perhaps the dog was not with him, for he was in a boat,
when he saw how the setting sun

> A lingering lustre softly throws
> On the dear hills where first he rose.

Wordsworth never forgot that setting sun; the lines about
it he put suggestively at the beginning of his collected
poems. They had become significant; as he looked back on
his boyhood days, he saw them strangely illuminated, not
by a light cast by a fond but false memory, but by their own
light, the vision splendid. Though on his reaching manhood
it faded away, it had become the fountain-light of all his
day and a master-light of all his seeing. The Child who was
father of the Man may have slashed the lady's hooped
petticoat, but he had also walked in an auroral vision.

At Cambridge Wordsworth must have felt farther from
the dear hills than the map suggests. He was not like
Coventry Patmore who preferred a flat country, mountains being to him "great impostors," "petrified catas-
trophes," "nothing heaped upon nothing."[1] That so much
of the earth was taken up by "greedy mountains" proved
to Lucretius that it had no Creator; Wordsworth said it
was among mountains that he *felt* his faith. And he took
no great interest in his studies, nor, apparently, in field
sports, if he imagined a crowd applauded when

> The inglorious foot-ball mounted to the pitch
> Of the lark's flight,—or shaped a rainbow curve,
> Aloft.

[1] *Hastings, Lewes, Rye and the Sussex Marshes.*

In spirit he was much in his "dear native Regions,"
writing *An Evening Walk,* his memory so clear that cows
standing in a lake he saw as "shorten'd herds." And to
Hawkshead he had to return for a memorable experience.
De Quincey and John Wilson wondered how the austere
Wordsworth could have relaxed enough to woo his wife;
but perhaps it was not difficult. Attending a dance, he had
his share of the "shocks of young love-liking," so full a
share that on his way home he felt

> The memory of one particular hour
> Doth here rise up against me.

The dawn was reproachful, but Nature herself took him
in hand:

> bond unknown to me
> Was given, that I should be, else sinning greatly,
> A dedicated Spirit.

He had gone to the dance in his Cambridge clothes,
"splendid" in the country girls' eyes; he returned even
better clothed in his own eyes, in "priestly robe." Nature's
choice of her priest was in some ways odd; in a poem about
the small celandine he confesses that for thirty years or
more he could not have named that common flower. But
no doubt Nature was right; he had a nephew who became
a bishop; Wordsworth in his different hierarchy rose to be
Primate of All England.

Some years passed, however, before he fully entered on
his priestly office, his mind too agitated by the French
Revolution. But at Racedown in Dorset, where he settled
down with his sister Dorothy, his mind also began to settle
down, while at the same time his spirits, depressed by a
lack of self-confidence, began to rise. Their house lay at the

foot of Pillsdon Pen. An easy ascent leads to its broad back which ends in a headland, crowned with a camp, where one gazes in wonder on Marshwood Vale. Beyond is Lewesdon Hill, the subject of a poem by William Crowe, which to Samuel Rogers was full of noble poetry, but to Wordsworth was "an excellent loco-descriptive poem." But all around Racedown is a sea of hills, stormy yet placid, stretching to the sea itself. Yet it was not charming scenery Dorothy had in mind when she wrote, "I think Racedown is the place dearest to my recollections upon the whole surface of the island"; she was thinking of her happiness in being again with her brother. And of something more, for De Quincey significantly points out that Dorothy means Gift of God. She helped William to recover his self-confidence; the bond given by Nature still held; he was a "dedicated Spirit." Yet Nature might not have approved of what we are told: "he relaxed the rigour of his philosophic nerves so much as to go a-Coursing"; one does not go coursing hares in a "priestly robe." His new friend Coleridge might have pointed out,

> He prayeth best, who loveth best
> All things both great and small.

When his cottage at Nether Stowey was overrun by mice, Coleridge felt it was unchivalrous to combat them with traps.

For the sake of Coleridge's company the Wordsworths moved to Holford, a hamlet in a combe of the Quantocks, exchanging a large house for a larger, Alfoxden. The Quantocks are modest hills, and yet two-faced; you can cross the range and view the dark forbidding outline of Exmoor and, returning, receive through the trees a warm welcome from Somerset's red ploughlands. If your crossing is in autumn, when heather and dwarf gorse mingle their purple and gold, you will see the hills in a regal splendour. If they lend themselves to poetic description, Wordsworth did not accept the loan. They provided him with subjects, but in a somewhat thankless way. It is not flattering to them that the story of *Simon Lee*, an Alfoxden man, is transferred to "the sweet shire of Cardigan." No one would know that on the Quantocks' ridge Wordsworth saw the dead tree that gave birth to *The Thorn*. Miss Fenwick was probably surprised when he told her that *Peter Bell* was suggested as he stood gazing at asses in Alfoxden Park, though the fact itself is not hard to believe. So Holford people have taken no pride in Wordsworth's association with Alfoxden House. A villager told Cottle "he had seen him wander about at night, and look strangely at the moon." The traditional memory of the Wordsworths, which lasted well into the present century, was that they were a queer pair who roamed about in the dark. They were only remembered because at the time their residence caused a sensation; the slouching, unsocial man and his so-called sister, brown as a berry, were French spies. Wordsworth gained the distinction, unusual for a poet, of being watched by a detective.

Coleridge often accompanied the Wordsworths on their night rambles; perhaps on one of them he heard in Holford Combe the hidden brook,

> That to the sleeping woods all night
> Singeth a quiet tune.

He discoursed much on Spinoza's philosophy, a subject not unsuited to the dark, if his exposition of it was, "Each thing has a life of its own, and we are all one life." Wordsworth's philosophy has a superficial resemblance to Spinoza's. He was an objective poet;

A primrose by a river's brim
A yellow primrose was to him;

"each thing has a life of its own." But while for Peter Bell
it was nothing more, an object in isolation, for Wordsworth it was, as he was himself, a selected point in the
mysterious surrounding presence of Nature; "we are all
one life." But his philosophy had an advantage over
Spinoza's in not needing thought or study. The "meddling
intellect" was out of place in a "breathing world";
indeed, "we murder to dissect." All that was needed was a
"wise passiveness." When his good friend Matthew asked
why, neglecting his books, he sat for half the day on an
old grey stone, he could reply,

"Think you, mid all this mighty sum
Of things for ever speaking,
That nothing of itself will come,
But we must still be seeking?"

But the Alfoxden poems give a trivial exposition of his
philosophy compared with *Tintern Abbey*. That poem, however, was written about a fortnight after the Wordsworths
were turned out of Alfoxden House.

In the preface to *The Excursion* Wordsworth gives some
account of his philosophy; when Blake read it, he became
ill. "It caused him a severe stomach complaint, which
nearly killed him."[1] Nature was the Devil's work and
Wordsworth an Atheist. Natural objects deadened &
obliterated the Imagination; the Corporial or Vegetative
Eye was like a window, not to be used for sight, but looked
thro'. On the other hand the *Immortality Ode* almost flung
him into a state of rapture; Wordsworth was the *only poet*
of the age. For the *Ode* described what Blake himself had

[1] Crabb Robinson, *Letter to Dorothy Wordsworth*.

experienced, the auroral vision; indeed, phenomenal creature, he had never lost it:

> I remain'd as a child;
> All I had ever known
> Before me bright shone.

In Wordsworth's poem *There was a Boy* occurs an obituary notice. After telling how through his hands the Boy

> Blew mimic hootings to the silent owls,

the poem states,

> This Boy was taken from his Mates, and died
> In childhood, ere he was full twelve years old.

But the boy was Wordsworth himself! The notice could refer only to the Child who was father of the Man, the growing Boy who walked in the auroral vision. W. H. Hudson thought Wordsworth read back into his childhood a visionary experience of later life, perhaps such an experience as he relates of himself: "this natural world was changed to a supernatural, and there was no more matter nor force in sea or land nor in the heavens above, but only spirit."[1] In the Western Highlands sea and land sometimes take on that immaterial appearance, but to one who has known them both it has no resemblance to the auroral vision. For Wordsworth the vision had become a boyhood memory. The cuckoo, the same he listened to in his schoolboy days, could bring back the memory,

> till I do beget
> That golden time again;

but the vision itself,

[1] *Afoot in England.*

Where is it now, the glory and the dream?

It is unfortunate that Wordsworth linked the auroral vision with the Platonic idea of a pre-existence; that he speaks of "taking hold of the idea" suggests that it was not relevant. Yet it was tempting to associate it in some way with Heaven, as, for example, to say,

Heaven lies about us in our infancy!

a pleasant thought in itself. Henry Vaughan almost so links it:

I cannot reach it; and my striving eye
Dazzles at it, as at eternity.

And Wordsworth's account of it is rich in ritualistic language: "apparelled in celestial light," "as to the tabor's sound,"

"My heart is at your festival,
My head hath its coronal,"

"glory," "priest," "imperial palace." "A splendour in the objects of sense" is how he describes the vision in prose. The same sense of splendour is suggested by Vaughan:

When on some *gilded Cloud*, or *floure*
My gazing soul would dwell an houre.

And by Traherne: "The corn was orient and immortal wheat, which never should be reaped, nor was ever sown . . . The dust and stones of the street were as precious as gold. . . . The green trees when I saw them first transported and ravished me, their sweetness and unusual beauty made my heart to leap. . . . Adam in Paradise had not more sweet and curious apprehensions of the world, than I when I was a child."[1] "Thou best philosopher,"

[1] *Centuries of Meditations.*

Wordsworth addresses the Child, but unfortunately a child cannot give a philosophical account of his experience. Unless we have seen it for ourselves, we cannot guess the significance of what those boys saw before sight became too subjected to its common utilitarian purpose, and useless perhaps for another purpose.

Haworth

HAWORTH might be thought the most interesting small town in England. Lying on the outskirts of an industrial district, almost a suburb of Keighley, it may prove unlike what you expected. You were prepared for that "one steep narrow street—so steep that the flag-stones with which it is paved are placed end-ways, that the horses' feet may have something to cling to, and not slip backwards";[1] but you may not have imagined a street of considerable beauty, rather austere, curious in the way it both repels and attracts. The houses are streaked with perennial soot, but in so peculiar a manner you might fancy the town was in half-mourning for those celebrated sisters, Charlotte and Emily Brontë. The new church, which keeps the old tower, is poor, but it has an astonishing graveyard, full of smoke-blackened flat tombstones, looking like tables spread with crape for a feast of ghosts. The small sedate parsonage, over-weighted with a new wing, has been turned into a museum, but in so agreeable a fashion that it comes alive again as a house. You might get the impression that the visitors were viewing furniture, pictures, books and what not, about to be sold by auction; that after all only the Reverend Patrick Brontë was dead, and the young ladies had gone out on the moor. Following them there, you are surprised by the moor itself, not grandly wild like most Yorkshire moors, just pleasantly so, cut up

[1] Mrs Gaskell, *The Life of Charlotte Brontë.*

by small green valleys and enlivened by call of grouse and
curlew. It is not forbidding as in *Wuthering Heights*, and
you can understand how it was said of the author, "Emily
was a child in spirit for glee and enjoyment; a spell of mischief lurked in her when out on the moor."[1] But it is extensive at least, making you imagine the sisters are somewhere
out of sight.

The queer unusual beauty of the town, suggesting little
change since the sisters' time, and the personal belongings
you see in the parsonage, give you the feeling they are
still about the place. When Matthew Arnold speaks of
May calling them forth

> Yearly awake to behold
> The opening summer, the sky,
> The shining moorland,[2]

you feel the insincerity of a merely poetic idea. Yet,
strangely enough, you cannot in Haworth quite shake off
a sense of their presence. Emily induces it more than
Charlotte, for she was the Visionary, as she calls herself,
open to receive a ghostly visitation:

> Burn, then, little lamp; glimmer straight and clear—
> Hush! a rustling wind stirs, methinks, the air;
> He for whom I wait, thus ever comes to me;
> Strange Power! I trust thy might; trust thou my constancy.

She is almost defiant about her right to entertain her guest:

> And am I wrong to worship where
> Faith cannot doubt, nor hope despair,
> Since my own soul can grant my prayer?

That this extraordinary woman was so receptive of her
guest,

[1] *Letter of Miss Ellen Nussey.*   [2] *Haworth Churchyard.*

> ever-present, phantom thing—
> My slave, my comrade, and my king,

somehow lays us open to receive from her more than a
memory of herself, a living impression. It makes Haworth
a strange place; no other town has its peculiar interest.

The Disraelis

BRADENHAM spreads its broad reddish brick front
across a hill slope, the windows gazing down on a wide
valley; it deserves its dignified position, for it is a fine
house, a pleasant contrast to the egregious Hughenden
with its pathetic park. Behind it a rising wood of tall
beeches heightens the hill, while in its twilit shelter holly-
trees keep Christmas and dark yews Lent. But for all he
saw of the charming scene Isaac Disraeli might as well
have stayed in London, for, as his son says, "he scarcely
ever left his room but to saunter in abstraction upon a
terrace." He may not have needed exercise, having adopted
as his motto, "The struggle for knowledge hath a pleasure
in it like that of wrestling with a fine woman." Yet he had
been a poet in his youth, so alarming his father that "the
loss of one of his argosies, uninsured, could not have filled
him with more blank dismay." He was packed off, "like
a bale of goods," to live with his father's correspondent in
Amsterdam, "where a new scene and a new language
might divert his mind from the ignominious pursuit." But
not till he was thirty-five did he renounce his "dreams."
And he had written a poem which kind-hearted Scott
warmly commended. He was pleased with it himself, and
included it in—*Curiosities of Literature.* Its subject might
not appeal to all present-day readers, the title being,
*Stanzas, addressed to Laura, entreating her not to paint or
powder.* Latterly he became blind, but he did not follow

Milton's example and write an epic; that was left to his son Benjamin.

Young Benjamin Disraeli must have delighted in Bradenham, for long after he left it he described it in *Endymion*, though calling it by a false name, Hurstley, and faithlessly removing it from the Chilterns to the Berkshire Downs. And he must have had a feeling for the surrounding country; even the Wye, a poor stream that gives its name to the low-lying town, High Wycombe, he affectionately called "that ancient river, the river Kishon." When on his father's death he came to buy a house for himself, he chose Hughenden, which was only a few miles away, though far beyond his means. Riding with the hounds, he would explore a wider area, a country of long low hills, naked to the sky or with a beech-wood like a cloak flung over them. Sheep and juniper bushes climb their gentle slopes, and among them lie small villages content to look old-fashioned. Diversity of soil gives the Chilterns a rich and varied vegetation, saving them from the monotony of some hills. They are also saved from it by being broken up, not so much by wide valleys, as by small partings, modestly called bottoms. Other things are on a small scale, farms, fields and orchards having a childlike look. Though the scene continually changes, the pedestrian has a feeling of intimacy with the Chilterns as with no other hills. Disraeli may have followed the hounds as far as their northern escarpment, where the view is so extensive that foreign diplomats, staying with later Prime Ministers at Chequers, must imagine they see half of England. It is still a lonely country, at least in parts, where the most you hear is the whining sound of a woodman's saw, which you might mistake for the despairing wail of a falling tree. But its quiet beauty may not have appealed to a young man who was a noted dandy and whose favourite bird was the peacock. It was to sublimer scenery, the Italian Alps, he turned in writing the epic.

The conception of this work came to him far from Bradenham, on the windy plain of Troy. "What!" he exclaimed, "is the revolution of France a less important event than the siege of Troy? Is Napoleon a less interesting character than Achilles? For me remains the Revolutionary Epick." Yet it was at Bradenham he felt the effervescing impulse to begin the work:

> On me descends the spirit of great song:
> A holy office mine, and noble aim.

And there most of it was accomplished. "Now nearly a year has elapsed. And what an eventful one!" Unfortunately Bradenham cannot claim to be the actual birthplace of the *Revolutionary Epick*; it was finished at Southend. It is from there he writes, "I await the great result with composure, though I am not sanguine of pleasing the million." But it did not even please his friends. To a writer who sent him one of his books, he replied, "Many thanks; I shall lose no time in reading it." His friends may have expressed their opinion of the *Epick* with a similar ambiguity.

John Clare

JOHN CLARE lies on the south side of Helpston churchyard, where the shadow of the chancel often falls; the
vicar, or whoever it was that laid him there, had not read
in his *Memorandum*, "I wish to lye on the North side of the
Churchyard, just about the middle of the ground where the
Morning and Evening Sun can linger longest on my
Grave." Clare's feeling for the sun was more than warm,
it was intimate. When he lost his bearings in unfamiliar
country, as at Newark, he fancied the sun had done the
same: "I was foolish enough to think the sun's course was
altered." Though Northborough was only three miles from
Helpston, when he went to live there he could say,

> The sun e'en seems to lose its way
> Nor knows the quarter it is in.

No doubt he loved the sun for its own sake; one might
gather that from his habit of sitting on mole-hills, "thymy
seats," "summer cushions"; these small Alps are as
common in his poems as in the Helpston meadows. But his
feeling must have been partly inspired by another feeling,
his love for all the small creatures that live by its light;

> For everything I felt a love,
> The weeds below, the birds above.

"Birds, bees, trees, flowers, all talked to me incessantly,
louder than the busy hum of men, and who so wise as

nature out of doors on the green grass by woods and streams under the beautiful sunny sky."

Helpston lies on the border of Fenland, a wide open country with an empty look. Distant trees stand on the earth's edge, almost falling over it; Clare set out as a boy to reach that edge, expecting to gaze down into a deep pit. Wet and incult, this may have been the part of Northamptonshire to which Hythodaeus refers, "the sheep are said to be so greedy and intractable that they eat up men, and depopulate fields, houses and whole towns."[1] Though it was being enclosed and cultivated in his time, Clare could say,

> The horses' footings with a sucking sound
> Fill up with water on the firmest ground.

An uninviting country, it may have encouraged him to pay attention to earth's small creatures. His poems are as alive with them as a summer's day. Indeed, he seldom lifts his eyes to view the landscape, though in one visionary picture he sees Fenland,

> A mighty flat, undwarfed by bush and tree,
> Spread its faint shadow of immensity.

Behind Helpston, as it were, are low wooded hills with open spaces, called Helpston Heath. Over these he used to ramble, especially on that day of rest from labour, the Sabbath, so often mentioned in his poems. "I got a bad name among the weekly church goers, forsaking the churchgoing bell and seeking the religion of the fields." The bad name he would not mind, but he was sensitive as to how people thought he was spending his time. As he was shy of revealing his love of poetry—returning from Stamford with a precious prize, Thomson's *Seasons*, he

[1] Sir Thomas More, *Utopia*.

M

climbed over the wall into Burghley Park to read it—so also he was shy of revealing his love of Nature. On his rambles on the Heath he liked to keep out of sight, hidden in woods,

> resting in the shade
> Of social loneliness.

If the inviting woods like the uninviting Fenland encouraged an interest in earth's small creatures, it would, indeed, be a social loneliness.

Perhaps his chief pleasure was in the society of plants; he went on the Heath

> to botanize
> And hunt the orchis tribes.

About a hundred and twenty different plants have been counted in his poems. He is expressing his own pride in their company when he says that every lane

> Triumphant boasts a garden of its own.

Some of his poems could make the same boast. It is not just their names we read; we see them for ourselves, noting how in the evening

> Daisies button into buds,

and how the holly bush smiles at winter

> With all the leafy luxury of May.

But he is also familiar with birds; of their characteristic flights he is more observant than the one-eyed camera:

> The crow goes flopping on from wood to wood,
> The wild duck wherries to the distant flood;
> Whizz goes the pewit o'er the ploughman's team,
> With many a whew and whirl and sudden scream.

With insects he is even more familiar. A strange Gulliver, he enters *The Insect World*, where totter-grasses are mighty oaks, rushy burnets as tall as castles, and every leaf a town. The insects admit him to their sleeping-chambers, the flower-bells; there he sees them

> like to princes in their chambers lie,
> Secure from night, and dropping dews, and all,
> In silken beds and roomy painted hall.

Clare shows his feeling for creatures that enjoy the sunlight by his sympathy with those that do not, even with the flowers that grow in woodland shade,

> And in its green light smile their lives away.

The frog is one of those creatures. "I love," he says, and it is a common beginning of a sentence,

> I love at early morn, from new-mown swath,
> To see the startled frog his route pursue,
> And mark while, leaping o'er the dripping path,
> His bright sides scatter dew.

But it does not get far, for speaking of the thousands of frogs he had seen crossing a common, he says, "as soon as the sun gets strong, they hide in the grass to wait the approach of night."[1] Then, of course, all is well,

> And all along the shaven mead,
> Jumping travellers, they proceed.

Then there is the jetty snail. This creature crawls over so many of his poems that he must have felt a special affection for it; you almost expect the name to be Jetty Snail, even with Miss affixed, for he would not know it was a hermaphrodite. It was one of those creatures that talked to him

[1] *Natural History Letters.*

louder than the busy hum of men; in fact, it was with the jetty snail specially in mind that he said, "Nature is a fine preacher and her sermons are always worth attention." The jetty snail preached on providence, and was itself the sermon, being a good example of a creature endowed with a providential instinct. "The instinct of the snail is very remarkable; it has such a knowledge of its own speed that it can get home to a moment to be safe from the sun as a moment too late would be its death." Unfortunately it does not practise what it preaches;

> Frail brother of the morn,
> That from the tiny bents and misted leaves
> Withdraws his timid horn,
> And fearful vision weaves,

it is too distrustful of providence. It is pleasant to think that in his asylum days Clare never lost his love of earth's wild creatures, and even wrote of them in a new and more lyrical way.

A love of that kind may lead to a religious experience. Clare found it so; "religion of the fields" was not for him a figure of speech:

> I feel a presence of delight and fear,
> Of love and majesty far off and near;
> Go where I will, its absence cannot be,
> And solitude and God are one to me.

These contrasts, "delight and fear," "far off and near," are signs of a sense of the numinous, or, as Clare puts it, "communings with God and not a word spoken." But as his mind lost its grip on reality, he came to have other communings. His love of Nature became fused with his love of poetry. The two were not far apart when he could say,

> I found my poems in the fields
> And only wrote them down,

or tell a visitor to the asylum, "I kicked them out of the clods." But the two were separate, and each had first to be fused with a third, his love of Mary Joyce.

School companion, "beloved with a romantic or Platonic sort of affection," she had passed out of his life; it was not Mary he married but Martha, whom he calls Patty. But alive or dead, she re-entered his life, a lady divinity, who appeared in dreams and, as he says, "left such a vivid picture of her visits in my sleep, dreaming of dreams, that I could no longer doubt her existence." She was the inspiring spirit of his poetry, "Mary, the muse of every song"; and also a presiding genius of Nature:

> The lost breeze kissed her bright blue eye,
> The bee kissed and went singing by.

She was even more, "for she was nature's self." This triune love was both his hope and despair:

> Thou fire and iceberg to an aching soul,
> And still an angel in my gloomy way;

but it was more a hope:

> In falsehood's enmity they lie
> Who sin and tell us love can die.

But at least it lifted him above his old self, the Nature-poet. Perhaps some sense of that made him tell people he was Lord Byron, believing it himself, and write a poem called *Childe Harold*. If Byron had the opportunity of reading his asylum poems in another world, where love is better understood, he may have welcomed him to it, slapping him on the back and saying, "Well done, John; I was far from grudging you my name; you did it a great honour."

Tennyson in Lincolnshire

SOMERSBY lies among hills, for in flat Lincolnshire the Wolds are hills. The place itself is hilly, the former Rectory in a hollow, the Church on a small eminence; the stream at the foot of the Parson's Field, no doubt the *Brook*, has to keep on running. There is little to remind one of Tennyson; a glass case in the Church shows two clay pipes he smoked, but not a bottle of port such as he drank daily. He must have been attached to these hills, for when he went to Cambridge he wrote, "the country is so disgustingly level." Looking back on them he saw

> A distant dearness in the hill,
> A secret sweetness in the stream.

Tennyson spent most of his life among hills, at Farringford on the Isle of Wight downs and at Aldworth on the Sussex Blackdown. He liked to wander on high places, sea-cliffs and mountains, and of these are some of his best descriptions. Though it was of a crag-perched eagle he said,

> The wrinkled sea beneath him crawls,

he may have remembered the sea-view as he stood on a Cornish cliff; a morning mist's peculiar way of climbing a mountain slope,

> The swimming vapour floats athwart the glen,
> Puts forth an arm, and creeps from pine to pine,
> And lingers, slowly drawn,

he may have noticed on one of his three ascents of Snowdon. Yet it is less with heights we associate his poems than with marshland flats and low sand-dunes, even parks with immemorial elms.

"Come down, O Maid, from yonder mountain height,"

he might have said to his Muse.

It is odd he found the Cambridge country disgustingly level, for most of Lincolnshire is so flat that it looks like a solid sea. Schooldays at Louth and holidays at Mable-thorpe had made it familiar to him from early youth, and living on the high Wolds it was continually under his eyes. But familiarity had not bred contempt; Lincolnshire scenes were in his mind when he wrote, "A known landskip is to me an old friend, and, indeed, does more for me than many an old friend." The flatness was in its favour; he could even declare, "The Lincolnshire marsh is as impressive in its extent of plain as mountain heights." If length impresses the eye as much as height, no doubt it is, for water-dykes stretch to the ends of the earth, even to infinity, their sides showing that parallel lines can meet. And land is the least part of the marsh; there is the whole encompassing sky, with superfluous bits spilt in the numerous ditches. And no part of England is more closely related to the sea; land and sea meet on level terms, at least to a large extent, nothing dividing them except low sand-dunes, which may be called neutral, being neither sea nor land.

Pictures of the marsh and coast are frequent in Tennyson's poems. Some are slight, a stanza or less:

> a tract of sand,
> And someone pacing there alone,
> Who paced for ever in a glimmering land,
> Lit by a low large moon.

In Tennyson's country the full moon rises oftener than once a month; indeed, you seldom visit it in his poems without seeing it rise. High among the clouds it may take to flying, but at first, a large heavy ball, it can hardly lift itself from the low horizon.

> The long noon wanes; the slow moon climbs; the deep
> Moans round with many voices;

the languid statement, "the slow moon climbs," impeding the line's flow, helps us to see its laboured rise. In *Mariana* there are two moons, one low, the other very low. The poem is a full-sized picture of a moated grange in the marsh. "With blackest moss," it begins, and though moss is not black, but usually a vivid green, the word suggests the scene, night-dark earth, dull stagnant water, glooming flats, even the white curtain swaying at the window. A peculiarity of the marsh is that single objects catch the eye, and in the picture we see a solitary poplar;

> For leagues around no other tree did mark
> The level waste.

In the refrain with its repeated "she only said" and "she said" we hear the monotonous sighs of rushes swaying to and fro. It was when he was talking about the poem that Tennyson declared that the marsh was as impressive as mountain scenery; certainly a scene that has so close a correspondence with Mariana's desolate feelings could not fail to be impressive in its melancholy way.

Tennyson was in the habit of making notes for later use, "nature-similes," some, no doubt, made only in memory. One of these notes is obvious in *The Dying Swan*, where it is out of place.

> The tangled water-courses slept,

we are told, and also,

> With an inner voice the river ran.

But only a swift stream plays that curious vocal trick; he
must have heard it, not in the marsh, but on the Wolds.
The chalky Wolds would also be a likely place to see the
fruit,

> Which in our winter woodlands looks a flower,

the spindle-tree's. This habit of making notes must have
sharpened his observation. Certainly some poets might
have found it helpful; Wordsworth did not distinguish
between an eyebright and a speedwell, and Matthew
Arnold thought a convolvulus climbed by means of tendrils.
Tennyson's observation was so good that many of his
readers would hardly have believed his eyesight was so
bad that he wore thick glasses; had he not opened their
own eyes? They had never noticed that a snowdrop's white
was streaked with green. Mr Holbrook confessed that he
had lived all his life in the country, but, old fool that he was,
he had not known that ash-buds were black till this young
man came and told him.[1] But the young man must have
left his glasses at home that day he saw,

> High-elbow'd grigs that leap in summer grass,

mistaking the grasshoppers' legs for arms. Yet glasses
might not have saved him from saying in the *Lady of
Shalott*,

> By the margin, willow-veil'd,
> Slide the heavy barges trail'd
> By slow horses.

He was married at Shiplake on the Thames, and though

[1] Mrs Gaskell, *Cranford*.

the wedding was, as he said, the nicest he had ever attended, he might have noticed that horses kept to the towpath, clear of willows.

It is unfortunate that his poems do not reveal something else about Tennyson, his affection for animals. His son says he inherited it from his mother; she was so tender-hearted towards animals that boys brought their dogs to her window and beat them till she gave them money to leave off. Though the *Brook* ran close to his home, Alfred could not bring himself to fish, and he greatly annoyed game-keepers by releasing animals from their traps. This affection would make him more sensitive to what he felt was Nature's cruelty: "her ravening tooth is a cruel one"; and also, for it was much akin, to what he felt was her waste: "the lavish profusion of the natural world appals me." These feelings raised problems in his mind. His usual way of escape from them was to dwell on Nature's outer charm,

> the satin-shining palm
> On sallows in the windy gleams of March,

or, the season even more congenial to him,

> autumn laying here and there
> A fiery finger on the leaves.

To escape was easy on the Wolds, but the marsh might almost accentuate the problems. Memories could endear it to him, but it is not an amiable country. Though highly cultivated, it retains a sullen look, showing that its native wildness is only suppressed; long straight dykes run across Lincoln Fen like restraining prison bars. The plough has tamed the fields, but water sulks in the dykes and ditches, and tall brown rushes wave with a defiant air. The marsh

has its minor charms, but Tennyson may not have found
them helpful;

> the silvery gossamers
> That twinkle into green and gold,

were spun by spiders. A rich harvest emphasised by its
economy the waste of thistledown, which filled the air with
what looked like ghosts but were still embryos, most of
which would perish.

Bishop Berkeley, as befitted a philosopher, took a more
cautious view of Nature's wastefulness: "We would do
well to examine, whether our taxing the waste of seeds
and embryos as an imprudence in the Author of nature, be
not the effect of prejudice contracted by our familiarity with
impotent and saving mortals."[1] Two later naturalists, who
distinguished themselves as writers, took a pleasanter view
of the life of animals than Tennyson; Richard Jefferies
could say, "The sense of living is manifestly intense in
them all, and is in itself an exquisite pleasure,"[2] while
W. H. Hudson regarded the idea that they live in a state
of fear as "a common pestilent delusion."[3] Julius Caesar
would not have criticised Nature for her "ravening tooth";
Plutarch tells that when he sat at table with friends and the
question was raised, which kind of death was the best, he,
answering before them all, cried out, "A sudden one."[4]

[1] *Principles of Human Knowledge.*
[2] *Wild Life in a Southern County.*
[3] *Birds in a Village.*   [4] *Lives* and *Moralia.*